# A word to the readers

We do not know what is happening to us, and this is precisely what is happening to us, not to know what is happening to us
José Ortega y Gasset

Human today has fallen into a terrible fire, which is called Alienation. Self-forgetfulness causes human to give up loving himself and not discover a reason for his existence. When he cannot discover the cause of his own existence, at certain moments he engages in actions that are often unintentionally anti-human. He does not know what action he is taking and he does not know whether this action was right or wrong in a situation where society has led human to depoliticize. He only acts and finds no reason for his actions. With a logic that considers truth dead and completely relativistic, that person will be more likely to justify his actions and will not seek the truth at all, or anything close to the truth. Human will not understand himself until he seeks to discover the closest thing to the truth, and human who does not know his individual identity will have no understanding of collective identity and Otherness. There is a close relationship between identity and truth. Without identity, there is no truth, and where there is no truth, anonymity shows itself.

The way forward for human is to think about the self. By looking at history, by taking refuge in art, by understanding philosophy, by perusing mythology and cultures, human can see his true face in the mirror and visualize another in the mirror.

The aim of Hermes Magazine is to present beauty and glory to its audience in the form of words, and by publishing the different ideas of writers from different countries and cultures, to some extent represent the true nature of human societies. We are very happy that you are the reader of this magazine and you are following us.

YOUR FRIEND,

*Mohammad Abedi*

# Contents

## Philosophy

## Literature

## Other Articles

# Poetry

# Short Story

Sᵗ Francis Bacon, Lord
Keeper and afterwards
Lord Chancellor of
England, 1617

# PHILOSOPHY

# FREEDOM AND EQUALITY

## BY THOMAS POGGE

Humanity's emancipation from feudalism was fought for and won under the twin banners of Freedom and Equality. The reaction against this emancipation has long sought to play these two values off against each other. It is said that, in a free society, people will make use of their freedoms in diverse ways, and this will inevitably lead to diversity of outcomes: to some being rich and others poor, some being much better educated, more powerful or more popular than others. Government can make people more equal. But the only way it can do so is by restricting their freedom: either by foreclosing their options to lead their lives as they choose, or through redistributive interference that erases the differences that emerge organically from citizens' free choices. Therefore, those who love freedom must accept inequality.

The present essay explores this anti-egalitarian reasoning and, more broadly, the relationship of freedom and equality. It does so by accepting, for the sake of argument, the proposed liberal principle: that freedom is the highest value. It then explicates this commitment with special attention to its implications for equality.

Liberalism posits that national societies and other social systems ought to be liberal, that is, ought to be structured to allow human beings to live as freely as possible.

The structuring here referred to has four interdependent components: ]

- the institutional order, centrally including the legally codified rules and practices of politics, family, work, commerce, finance, education, and health care;
- the social and cultural practices, customs, and habits that, even if not codified in law, profoundly affect human lives, as illustrated by the historically most important examples of racism, sexism and religious discrimination;
- the existing infrastructure, including traffic arteries for the movement of people and goods, cables and pipelines for energy and water supply, and communication channels for news, social media, and personal interactions;
- the physical environment as shaped and continuously changed by how human beings interact with it through settlements, agriculture, mining, sewage and emissions, landfills and formative uses of forests, meadows, lakes, rivers, coasts, parks, mountain ranges, and the like.

These structures have profound effects – not merely on what people can be, can have or can do, but also on their character, personality, and ambitions. Human beings structure, shape and design their own lifeworld. How they do so is of the greatest moral importance.

This how covers two different questions – about the design processes and the design outcomes.

Liberalism addresses both. Human beings ought to have formative freedom to participate in structuring their lifeworld. And this lifeworld ought to be structured so that human beings – protected against deprivation, stress and oppression – have a wide variety of attractive conduct options and choices about how to lead their lives.

This explication immediately highlights the central tension in liberalism: liberal design processes do not necessarily lead to liberal outcomes and may even undermine the liberal character of those design processes themselves. Historically, liberalism has often lost by not defending its own prerequisites hard enough, living up to Robert Frost's humorous definition of a liberal as someone "too broadminded to take his own side in a quarrel."[1] When some people use their legitimate formative freedoms in ways that threaten to deprive others of their formative freedom or their opportunity to live freely, then liberals must speak out forcefully on behalf of the latter – against enabling legislation,[2] against capture of politics by financial and business elites, against a globalization that squeezes all nations into one commercial monoculture, against extreme economic inequalities that force human beings into oppressive labor relations and deny their children the chance for education and full participation in economic and civic life.

In the first third of the long American Century, President Franklin D. Roosevelt committed the United States to liberalism in his famous Four Freedoms speech of 6 January 1941: "In the future days, which we seek to make secure, we look forward to a world founded upon four essential human freedoms. The first is freedom of speech and expression – everywhere in the world. The second is freedom of every person to worship God in his own way – everywhere in the world. The third is freedom from want – which, translated into world terms, means economic understandings which will secure to every nation a healthy peacetime life for its inhabitants – everywhere in the world. The fourth is freedom from fear – which, translated into world terms, means a world-wide reduction of armaments to such a point and in such a thorough fashion that no nation will be in a position to commit an act of physical aggression against any neighbor – anywhere in the world."[3] Toward the end of that American Century, the prospects of human beings for a life in freedom are slim. Even in regard to prosperity, which was touted as the strong suit of American liberalism, the situation is appalling. While the global average income has reached the purchasing power of USD 50 per person per day, this prosperity is extremely unevenly distributed: only about 7% of humankind reach the average level; and 41.9% cannot afford a healthy diet, estimated to cost (again, at purchasing power parity) USD 4.04 per person per day.[4] This shocking percentage describes 2019 – before the COVID pandemic struck and, amplified by the climate crisis, triggered a spike in food prices of 39% above general inflation.[5] Despite a very substantial increase in aggregate global prosperity, the American Century left half of humanity in abject poverty and precarity. These billions of human beings are denied a life in freedom: they suffer deprivation, stress, and oppression; their life choices and conduct options are extremely constrained; and they have, at best, very limited opportunities to play a formative role in structuring their lifeworld and environment.

One might say that this lack of freedom of half of humankind must be accepted because it results from free structuring decisions – by rich and powerful states, corporations, and individuals. But this defense of the status quo runs into two problems.

One problem is that this defense invokes an elite's really existing formative freedom that, according to the critique, should never have existed. Participation in shaping the human world is, crudely put, a constant-sum game: If some play a dominant role in structuring our lifeworld, then others must be confined to a less-than-equal role. One might think that this freedom deficit of the marginalized is acceptable because it is compensated by a freedom surplus of the privileged. But two thoughts undermine this opinion. First, the diminishing marginal value of freedom: being able to participate meaningfully at all is of much greater importance than being able to do so to an above-average degree. Second, the universalizability principle (Kant etc.): freedom that is incompatible with a like freedom of others has no moral value.

This argument is supported by another. A small minority, thanks to its economic-military supremacy, has managed to structure the world so that it continuously reproduces massive poverty and extreme inequality. A large majority of humanity wills instead alternative structures under which most or all human beings would have much greater freedom of action and of formative participation. The structuring of the one world in which we all live cannot conform to the will of both sides. Positing freedom as the highest value favors, in case of conflict, making the structuring of our world conform to the will and judgment of the majority rather than that of a minority. Like the first, this second argument supports the conclusion that the minority has seized a hugely disproportionate formative freedom that it is not morally entitled to.

A further problem with the proposed defense of the status quo concerns not the design process but the design outcome. Here, liberalism cares about how alternative structurings of the world would affect the freedom of conduct and the formative freedom of all affected persons. As liberals, we ask: "Where should formative freedom – no matter who exercises it – find its limits?" With freedom as our highest value, we are opposed to anyone using her formative freedom in ways that undermine or even destroy the legitimate freedom of others (or her own future freedom). In such cases of conflict, balancing is needed. In this regard, the liberal tradition is agreed that formative freedom must be restricted in some cases: there must be no slavery, even if a majority wills it and even if those affected want to become, or indeed have become, slaves by their own free decisions. [6] The critique of the status quo says the same about severe poverty: it must be avoided, insofar as possible, because it severely constrains a person's freedom of action, freedom to lead one's own life and freedom to participate in shaping one's environment.

We now have three indications that our world, assessed from a liberal standpoint, is poorly structured:

- The present structuring deprives a large majority of human beings of their formative freedom to participate in shaping their environment.
- The present structuring of the world leaves a large majority of human beings little freedom of action, making it extremely difficult for them to free themselves from deprivation, stress and oppression, and offers them no attractive options to shape their own life.
- The world's present structuring does not correspond to the will and judgment of most human beings. The currently marginalized majority aspires to a greater, ultimately an equal formative role in structuring our world and to greater freedom of life and action. There is moral value in one's lifeworld being consistent with one's will and judgment, in this lifeworld being structured as one wills it to be and judges it right. This value of being reconciled with one's social world is emphasized especially by Hegel as central to human freedom.[7]

All three points relate, in different ways, to equality. But this is not some independent principle of equality to be weighed against the demand for freedom. Rather, the idea is that everyone's freedom is valuable and ought to be equally taken into account in structuring decisions – the freedom of women no less than that of men, the freedom of workers no less than that of entrepreneurs, the freedom of Africans no less than that of Europeans.

In our world, by far the greatest deficits in freedom are linked to poverty. This is true nationally, even in the richer countries, and especially globally. Those who must struggle and fear every day about feeding their families are exposed to deprivation, stress and oppression and have minimal opportunities to shape their own life and to participate in structuring their environment. This does not have to be so, as can be shown through three possible restructurings.

The current structuring of the world gives people considerable freedom in the exploitation of natural resources. Anyone who can bring himself to power in a country – even by force – can enrich himself by creating legally valid property rights in this country's natural resources, and any state can abuse the atmosphere and oceans at will for emissions and waste of all kinds. These activities lead to massive devaluation of our planet: natural resources are depleted, the climate deteriorates, air and water pollution endanger humans and all living beings. While in principle everyone is free to participate in this destructive overexploitation, in reality it is only a minority of wealthy people who can take advantage of this freedom.[8]

A better arrangement would be at least to compensate poor people for this planetary loss of value by transferring part of the privately appropriated or (by polluting emissions) depreciated value to the excluded people in the form of a basic dividend. The resulting increased costs of exploitation would accelerate the urgently needed green transformation of the world economy; and the basic dividend of 2–3% of world product would immediately eradicate at least the severe forms and manifestations of poverty.[9] The gain in freedom would be enormous, the loss in freedom – subjective and moral – no more than minor.

A second example involves innovation incentives. Currently, innovation is rewarded worldwide by 20-year monopoly patents that allow patent holders to charge high markups or royalties – with the result that pharmaceuticals, for example, are often sold at over 1000 times the cost of production and therefore inaccessible to many. In 2013, a good drug against hepatitis C finally came on the market – in the U.S. at a price of $84,000 per 84 pills.[10] Four years after its launch, this drug – due to its high price – had reached only 7% of relevant patients worldwide. The remaining 66 million predominantly poorer hepatitis C patients remain ill and continuously infect other people in their vicinity (to the benefit of the patentee!).[11] One can hardly console these unserved patients with the fact that they also have the right to invent drugs, patent them around the world and then sell them at monopoly prices because, in reality, they lack this freedom.

It would be much better to reward important innovations with publicly funded impact rewards: a new medicine according to the health gains achieved with it, a new green technology according to the emission reductions achieved with it, and so on. Freed from monopoly markups, innovations would then be accessible not only to a wealthy minority, but would spread rapidly around the world, with large gains for global health and climate. And innovators would have incentives to tackle problems concentrated among the poor – the many diseases of poverty, for example, which are now largely ignored by the pharmaceutical industry precisely because poor people cannot afford exorbitant monopoly markups. With health impact rewards, diseases like tuberculosis and malaria would become highly lucrative fields of pharmacological research.[12]

A third example is education. Today, half of all children receive only a minimal education, and 160 million children between 5 and 17 are engaged in wage labor outside their own households and thus do not go to school at all.[13] For these children, this means a severe, lifelong loss of freedom – and for the world it means a gigantic loss of talent and creativity. This goes on while the costs of worldwide primary and secondary education could probably be covered quite easily out of additional tax revenues from the resulting productivity gains in the world economy so that, overall, it would cost nothing to enable all children in this world to exercise the freedom to make meaningful choices about their life and conduct as well as the formative freedom to participate in shaping their environment to the best of their ability, judgment and will.

Each of these three reforms, and much more so all three of them together, would enormously enhance the freedom enjoyed by the poorer half of humanity. But liberalism, especially in Anglophone countries, is often pressed into the service of opposing such reforms on the ground that they would diminish, and also constrain the exercise of, the formative freedom of the most privileged and powerful states, corporations and individuals, who ought to be allowed to take full advantage of the formative freedom made possible by their enormous wealth and power, even when they use this freedom to subject poorer people to their will, in politics, economics, finance and culture.

According to the conception of liberalism here presented, the existing inequalities in wealth, power and formative freedom should never have been allowed to emerge because they result from a structuring that also produces extremely large freedom deficits for a majority of humankind. Liberalism must oppose such freedom deficits in favor of a structuring that would sustainably afford all human beings a genuine opportunity to live in freedom.

## Endnotes

[1] https://www.barrypopik.com/index.php/new_york_city/entry/a_liberal_is_a_man_too_broad_minded_to_take_his_own_side_in_a_quarrel/

[2] The paradigm example is the Ermächtigungsgesetz of 23 March 1933 – officially titled Law to Remedy the Distress of the People and the State – with which Germany's Parliament democratically abolished democracy by transferring most of its powers to Chancellor Adolf Hitler.

[3] https://www.ourdocuments.gov/doc.php?flash=false&doc=70&page=transcript

[4] FAO, IFAD, UNICEF, WFP and WHO (2021). The State of Food Security and Nutrition in the World 2021. Transforming Food Systems for Food Security, Improved Nutrition and Affordable Healthy Diets for All (Rome: UN Food and Agriculture Organization), https://doi.org/10.4060/cb4474en, Table 5, p. 27. Table 4, p. 18, shows that the number of human beings affected by nutritional deficits has increased every year since 2014, by about one half overall.

[5] The FAO's real (inflation-adjusted) food price index was 95.6 in 2019 and 132.7 in January 2022. See https://www.fao.org/worldfoodsituation/foodpricesindex/en/

[6] Nozick advocates slavery and, for this and other reasons, is not a liberal. See Robert Nozick (1974). Anarchy, State, and Utopia (New York: Basic Books), p. 331.

[7] This idea is found, for example, toward the end of the preface to Georg Wilhelm Friedrich Hegel (1991). Elements of the Philosophy of Right (Cambridge: Cambridge University Press), pp. 22–23.

[8] It is estimated that human beings in the poorer half, who are suffering the most from the effects of climate change, are responsible for about 7% of anthropogenic emissions, while the richest 10% are responsible for about half, the richest 1% of human beings for about 15%, and the richest 0.1% for about 4.5% of all greenhouse gas emissions. https://www.theguardian.com/environment/2022/feb/04/carbon-footprint-gap-between-rich-poor-expanding-study

[9] "A Global Resources Dividend." Chapter 8 in Thomas Pogge (2008). World Poverty and Human Rights: Cosmopolitan Responsibilities and Reforms (Cambridge, Polity Press).

[10] Barber, M. J., Gotham, D., Khwairakpam, G., & Hill, A. (2020). "Price of a Hepatitis C Cure: Cost of Production and Current Prices for Direct-Acting Antivirals in 50 Countries." Journal of Virus Eradication 6(3). https://doi.org/10.1016/j.jve.2020.06.001

[11]    Clinton    Health    Access    Initiative    (2020).    Hepatitis    C    Market    Report, https://3cdmh310dov3470e6x160esb-wpengine.netdna-ssl.com/wp-content/uploads/2020/05/Hepatitis-C-Market-Report_Issue-1_Web.pdf

[12] Thomas Pogge (2009). "The Health Impact Fund and Its Justification by Appeal to Human Rights." In Human Rights: Normative Requirements and Institutional Constraints, special issue edited by Andreas Follesdal, Thomas Pogge and Carol C. Gould of the Journal of Social Philosophy 40(4), pp. 542–569, http://onlinelibrary.wiley.com/doi/10.1111/j.1467-9833.2009.01470.x/abstract. An analogous proposal for the green technology sector is described in Thomas Pogge (2021). "GIFT or Gates?" Hermes Magazine 6, pp. 1–8. See also https://globaljustice.yale.edu/green-impact-fund-technology.

[13] ILO and UNICEF (2021). Child Labor: Global Estimates 2020, Trends and the Road Forward (Geneva and New York: International Labour Organization and United Nations Children's Fund), https://www.ilo.org/ipec/Informationresources/WCMS_797515/lang--en.

# LITERATURE

# THE STRANGE GIRL AND THE PERFECTED WOMAN

## BY STEPHANIE MARRIE

Sylvia Plath wrote "Cinderella" and "Edge" several years apart. However, she injects her struggle with society's idea of femininity – be it the pretty princess or the loving mother - into both of them. Plath's struggle is expressed differently according to the period of her life in which each poem was written. Despite writing both "Cinderella" and "Edge" in the third person, Plath and each of her speakers are one and the same. Due to her reputation as a confessional poet, all of Plath's work is autobiographical at source (Stevenson 2). Plath wrote "Cinderella" in 1952 during her juvenilia. In this period, her "tightly controlled" poems navigate the constraints of fifties' girlhood through fractured fairy tales (Spivack). The poems written in her post-Juvenilia period, on the other hand, are marked by fragmented self-exploration of a troubled life that included several miscarriages. Plath's 1963 swan song "Edge" is the shining example of her poetic self-exploration (Stevenson 2). When "Cinderella" and "Edge" are put side by side, what results from the clash between their respective periods is not the breakdown of control, already present in both poems, but the deconstruction of the woman – thematically and formally. The difference between them, though, is that the girl in "Cinderella" is made more approachable despite her inability to be a princess while the woman in "Edge" is withdrawn through her deviation from the caring mother.

At first, "Cinderella" presents the supposed American girl dream in all its sexist implications: winning a prince's love through her beauty. After all, this poem was written not long after Walt Disney put forth his glamorous heroine of the same name as a role model for an entire nation of girls in 1950. Unlike the Disney film, padded by the antics of mice, Plath skips over the first half of the story and begins right at the ball. The first words are, "The prince," which gets to a romantic girl's favorite part of the story right away. Plath betrays the fairy tale's gender roles at the outset. Only Cinderella is described in terms of how she looks, not the prince. The reader knows that she wears "scarlet heels" and has "green eyes" (lines 1-2). Plath does not reveal what the prince is wearing, nor does she describe what his face looks like. There are no allusions to how handsome the prince is, which implies that beauty is a trait specific to girls. The poem's iambic pentameter also betrays the story's gender roles by placing boy and girl on an unequal plane. The long stress falls on the word "prince" and then on "girl," (line 1). This implies that the prince comes first and the girl two steps behind of him in terms of importance. Despite the prince being the center of the girl's fantasy, the girl is the objectified center of attention in the first stanza.

"Cinderella" is built like a traditional sonnet both formally and thematically; therefore, it objectifies the girl. In the first three lines of the first quatrain, she is defined not by her character but by her appearance. The iambic long stress makes the girl out to be a mere sum of pretty parts instead of a whole person, falling on the words "heels, "green," "fan," and the first syllable of "silver," (lines 1-3). By not revealing the girl's skin color, Plath makes her a blank canvas to be given color and definition by her "scarlet heels" (line 1). The long stress augments the power of the shoes to define the girl by falling on the first syllable of "scarlet" and then on "heels" (line 1). Though Plath's description of Cinderella is built like a blazon, there is no male speaker to admire the girl, but instead a woman looking at herself the way a man would. Plath frames Cinderella's objectification this way to expose how pervasive the male gaze is in the traditional sonnet.

Despite the formality of the ball, "Cinderella" suggests that the ideal girl is sexually receptive. The words "fan" and "span" rhyme, thus emphasizing the girl's ability to open up (lines 2, 4). The fan, with its many folds and its ability to open, is the closest thing the poem has to a vagina. The girl opens her fan after the prince "leans" toward her and the violins are about to play (line 1). On this cue, the girl and the prince are about to make beautiful music together in more ways than one. The girl does not move toward the prince, she is not an active agent in her own courtship. However, when she senses that midnight threatens her chance with the prince, she "clings" to him (line 12). Though the girl now touches the prince, the word "cling" makes her seem scared and dependent. If Plath had used the word "attacked" or "caressed" instead, she would have made the girl more sexually dominant than the prince. The girl may not assert herself, but her passivity will not stop the fairy godmother's deadline from transforming her back into a scullery maid.

Towards the end of the poem, Plath fractures the feminine dream by suggesting the girl's inability to sustain it. Firstly, she turns the dream into a nightmare by rendering the ball unappealing. The guests, previously portrayed as graceful in terms such as "gliding into the light like wine" are now busybodies engaging in "cocktail talk" (line 6, 13). The music, previously described in elegant terms such as "rondo slows" is now an unwelcome, "hectic" distraction to the girl from all-important ticking clock (line 13). The specter of midnight looms in the middle of the third stanza: "Until near twelve the strange girl all at once / Guilt-stricken halts, pales, clings to the prince" (lines 11-12). It is close to twelve. It is unclear what the girl is feeling guilty for, whether it be deceiving the prince or staying out past midnight. Plath manages to imply the terrifying prospect of being revealed to everyone at the ball as a phony in a controlled manner despite losing the rhythm that made the first stanza move like a traditional sonnet.

From a structural standpoint, Plath heightens the fracturing of Cinderella's one night of happiness by abandoning the tempo of the dance in favor of the clock's ticking. For example, the rhyming words in the third stanza are not all the perfect rhymes of the first stanza. Though "since" and "prince" rhyme perfectly, "trance" and "once" are syllabic rhyme. The reader can also feel that this is the point where the music stops. Now, the rhythm of the line is no longer a regular iambic pentameter. Just as the syllable count gets messed up, the music loses its rondo, its previous tempo, and becomes "hectic" (line 13). The threshold between fantasy and grim reality occurs in line eleven, which happens to be one hour before the midnight deadline. Then the twelfth line concludes the terrifying thought that the eleventh line began. The reader can feel the clock tick from eleven to twelve, making it easier to understand the girl's increasing apprehension. By reading from the eleventh line to the twelfth line, the reader ticks the clock forward one hour just as Time marches on unrelenting.

The girl clashes with her former beautiful self, just as the author's power clashes with the girl's. No longer the belle of the ball, she is now a "strange" girl (line 11). The fact that she "pales" means that she fears the deadline because of what it means for her public reputation (line 12). This clash is what Elizabeth Wanning Harries, a twentieth-century feminist critic of the fairy tale, would call, "the problem of competing, even conflicting selves...woven out of different material exigencies and discursive possibilities," which fractured the fairy tale and allowed postmodern female writers like Plath to demonstrate "how such stories have both limited opportunities for girls and facilitated the development of young female readers into serious artists" (McCort 110, 175). In this case, Plath acknowledges that Cinderella's pedestal is a standard too high for an ordinary girl like her; therefore, it is inevitable that she will fall short and be denigrated for it. In order to escape the princess box, Plath has resolved to turn this sexist story into a subversive work of art. The poem's Cinderella may be confined in all her finery to the ballroom, but Plath channels Cinderella's inner discontent out from the lines and into the reader's head. However, while the girl in "Cinderella" has much to lose in the way of reputation, the protagonist of "Edge" has nothing to lose.

The poem "Edge," written six days before Plath's suicide, presents a resigned yet confident woman who puts herself before her children. This deviation from the ideal mother makes the first line, "The woman is perfected," ironic. The "Greek necessity" flowing "in the scrolls of her toga," is an allusion to the ritual suicides required of "disgraced individuals in the classical world" (Safya). If this is the case, then the woman's disgrace, and by extension Plath's, is her miscarriage. However, Plath suggests in the middle of the poem that the woman is not ashamed of her inability to nourish children but proud of it.

Plath reverses the loss of agency that a miscarriage entails by turning it into an active abortion. She justifies the abortion by demonizing the children, calling each one "a white serpent," (line 9). Instead of providing them with her breast milk, the woman lets them die of thirst by leaving them with an empty milk pitcher. The woman in "Edge" finds her identity precisely in her inability to conform to the ideal gender role and fears nothing, unlike her younger counterpart in "Cinderella." If the woman cannot succeed at becoming a proper mother, then she can rebel by becoming an improper mother. She "folds" her dead children "back into her body as petals / Of a rose close" (lines 12-14). The rose, with its many folds and its red color, is another vagina. Here, the woman closes in a sexual sense, not opens, unlike the girl in "Cinderella." She will not be receptive to a father or to the world, unlike Cinderella. Instead, she will listen to her feet when they say, "it is over," and take her children with her to the grave (line 8). Plath ends her subject's life in this way without regard to how repulsive the reader may find the woman as a human being, let alone a mother.

What the woman in "Edge" lacks in maternal qualities, she makes up for in patriarchal ones. When Plath mentions "A Greek necessity" and "scrolls" in the fourth and fifth lines, she also alludes to the study of the classics in order to commend the woman for fulfilling an intellectual ideal that had been previously assumed by wealthy male students. Scrolls are what contain most of the information from the ancient days. A Greek male scholar or public speaker also traditionally wears a toga. The woman who wears them here has a "smile of accomplishment" on her face (line 3). The reader is not given her looks or her accessories, unlike Cinderella. The woman's clothes are described, just like Cinderella's, but the "scrolls of her toga," suggest something more substantive than beauty (line 5). Therefore, Plath turns a woman who is not a traditionally ideal woman and turns her into a traditionally ideal man. By ascribing the traditionally masculine onto the woman, Plath makes her a more imposing figure.

To complement its woman, the poem "Edge" is blunt, unfeminine, and out of control from the outset. It is in free verse, and is not an elegant sonnet. There is no flowery language here, only grotesque imagery. The language involving flowers used always has something disgusting about it. For example, after the woman's rose closes, the garden "Stiffens and odors bleed," (line 15). The garden stiffening implies that its plants grow rotten, shrivel up, and die as mere brown twigs. When the speaker says that the odors bleed out of the "deep throats of the night flower," she means that the flower's sweet fragrance goes away from the flower (line 16). Not only is the imagery weird, but also the pacing is weird. Most of the couplets are fragmentary. Often, the first line of a couplet will be one sentence, and then the second line will begin a phrase that is completed in the first line of the next stanza. For example, the first couples of lines go, "The women is perfected. / Her dead / Body wears the smile of accomplishment" (1-3). The first couplet's pacing suggests the woman despairs at her state as an aberration to society and lashes out confusedly. The "unexpected enjambments" at the end of each couplet heighten the impression that the narrator is "disordered and unbalanced" (Safya). The unbalanced rhythm from stanza to stanza highlights the separation between subject and speaker. The woman may be smiling but the narrator is in anguish. The third stanza begins by hinting at the woman's intellectual achievement in the word "scrolls" yet ends with the beginning of a new topic – "Her bare" or vulnerable state – that will be continued as brusquely as a large foot squashing a bug by the next line's "Feet" (lines 5-7). Each time one phrase jumps to the next line of the next stanza, it feels like the speaker is struggling to catch her breath as she runs her agitated mouth off.

Nevertheless through the frenzied pace and the reversal of the girl on the pedestal, Plath uses "Edge" to come to terms with her deviation from her gender role regardless of the reader's opinion. Though both poems tackle a woman's struggles, "Cinderella" is evidently a poem written for an audience while "Edge" is written for Plath alone. Any girl can slip into the role of Cinderella, but only Plath can slip into the role of a disturbed and unwilling mother.

## Works Cited

McCort, Jessica Hritz. "Alice in Cambridge: Sylvia Plath, Little Girls Lost, and "Stone Boy with Dolphin"." Plath Profiles: An Interdisciplinary Journal for Sylvia Plath Studies 7 (2014): 175-86. Scholarworks. Google Scholar, 2014. Web. 9 Mar. 2015. <scholarworks.iu.edu>.

Safya, Ana. "Re: The Poetry of Sylvia Plath." Web log comment. EDGE by Sylvia Plath: Edge. Amazon Deals, July 2010. Web. 09 Mar. 2015.

Spivack, Kathleen. "Some Thoughts on Sylvia Plath." Rev. of Journals. Virginia Quarterly Review Spring 2004: n. pag. Some Thoughts on Sylvia Plath. VQR, 2015. Web. 19 Mar. 2015. <http://www.vqronline.org/essay/some-thoughts-sylvia-plath>.

Stevenson, Anne. "Sylvia Plath: The Illusion of a Greek Necessity." Sylvia Plath: The Illusion of a Greek Necessity (2013): 1-13. Anne Stevenson - Writer & Poet. Faber and Faber, 13 July 2013. Web. 9 Mar. 2015. <www.anne-stevenson.co.uk>.

# BALZAC: THE REALIST-VISIONARY CONUNDRUM

## BY CAMERON MANLEY

The 'querelle Balzac réaliste-Balzac visionnaire [Balzac as realist, Balzac as visionary dispute]' has been discussed by various critics, such as Goulet and Bays, the latter arguing that Balzac is both observateur [observer] 'who looked at the world with the exact eye of the scientist' as well as visionary 'who gazed [...] into the depths of the human spirit and beyond'. Balzac's relationship with historical truth seems to vary between incredibly simple (he is the heir of Scott's historical novel) and indefinably complex (sometimes considering himself an 'historien [historian]' (ii, 264), sometimes the 'secretaire [secretary]' (i, 264) of Parisian society, and at other times neither). However, in his Avant- propos Balzac writes 'J'ai fait mieux que l'historien, je suis plus libre [I've exceeded the historian, I am freer]' (i, 15). History, for Balzac, was not simply a series of historical events but also 'l'histoire oubliée par tant d'historiens, celle des mœurs [the history forgotten by so many historians, that of mores]' (i, 11). From historical facts of manners and mores, Balzac could draw a fictional verisimilitude. There is thus a difference between what is historically vrai [true] and what is fictionally vraisemblable [believable], the latter's function 'to reflect and reinforce a particular society's habitual definitions of reality'. In this sense the fictional may be based in reality, in the vrai, but extrapolated in order to reveal, not, as Herrera says, the obvious 'Histoire officielle [official history]', but an 'Histoire secrète [secret history]' ("H" majuscule) (v, 695), made up of hundreds, if not thousands, of individual petites histoires [mini-histories] ("h" miniscule). Balzac's intention to reveal the 'Histoire secrète' stemmed not from one particular character or event, but from the 'esprit d'une époque [the spirit of an age]' (viii, 897). The 'exactitude [precision]' (viii, 897) mentioned in the preface to Les Chouans [The Chouans], or even his Realist mission in general, was less depicting the vrai of historic details, which would limit 'liberté de la pensée [freedom of the thought]' (viii, 897), but in creating a novelistic vérité [reality] by synthesising the analytical details of the vrai [truth].

When looking at Balzac's Comédie humaine, there are in fact very few historical novels in the traditional sense. Whilst examples such as Adieu or Les proscrits do merit analysis, for the sake of this essay, I shall focus on Les Chouans, given that it is the first work to which Balzac put his real name. This novel takes its inspiration from the revolt in the Vendée. Contemporary terms such as 'les bleus [the blues]' (viii, 934) referring to republicans and explanations of terms such as 'le Gars' (viii, 917) (sobriquet of the Royalist leader Montauran), where we are told 'le mot gars, que l'on pronounce gâ, est un debris de la langue celtique [the word gars, which is pronounced ga, is leftover from celtic language]' (viii, 917) are included in order to faithfully recreate history. The narrator also describes in a way that was apt for the time: 'Dans les premiers jours de l'an VIII, au commencement de vendémiaire [In the first days of year VIII, at the start of Vendémiaire]' (viii, 906) before translating this into a date familiar to modern readers: 'pour se conformer au calendrier actuel, vers la fin du mois de septembre 1799 [to conform to the modern calander, the end of the month of September 1799]' (viii, 906). The narrator thereby links the past to the present and makes history itself a subjective entity, emphasising the spurious nature of the 'Histoire officielle' and, as shall be demonstrated, positing the 'petites histoires' of each individual and their perception of history as key. In this case, for the Republicans involved, history was increasingly understood as a current event created by the acts of individuals, but the monarchist reader (and writer) sees it differently: as degradation. This reflects the contrast made by Vigny, one of Balzac's contemporaries, between Vérité de l'Art [Reality of art] and Vrai du Fait [Truth of fact], between the essence of things and their appearances in fiction. Balzac ostensibly merges two different perceptions of history so that whilst not every detail corresponds mechanically to an exact historical fact, as this would kill artistic invention, there is a perception of history.

Balzac's desire to observe and record his own society in action meant that his focus was never fully drawn to 'history' as past, but a desire to explore the present and the 'creative energy that would propel society into the future'. Furthermore, he tells us in Sur Catherine de Médicis [On Catherine of Medicis] that 'Nous pouvons voir, par ce qui se passe de nos jours, que l'histoire se fasse au moment même où elle se fait [We can see from what happens nowadays that history is made in the moment that it occurs]' (xi, 199). He considered the linear model of history, as constant progression from a fixed point in the past, incorrect. True history encompassed history's dynamism and as he himself developed as a writer, the gap between date of story and date of publication decreases from 30 years between Les Chouans' setting in 1799 and publication in 1829, until with La Cousine Bette [Cousin Bette] and Le Cousin Pons [Cousin Pons] he attempts to capture history in the present moment. Indeed, Lousteau tells Lucien in Illusions perdues [Lost Illusions] that 'Le roman à la Walter Scott est un genre et non un système [the novel à la Walter Scott is a genre and not a system]' (v, 443). Whilst Scott organised his novels in the sense of tales and Rob Roy, Waverly and Redgauntlet, say, reflect a progression of different periods of Scottish history, they remain independent stories. Balzac, however, pushes this further through the creation of an entire system in the Comédie and depicts the impact of social change on characters' lives.

Balzac's use of recurring characters thus develops this idea of subjectivity and 'système [system]' as what we receive is more a snapshot of a character's life at different points rather than a complete account. Take as an example Hulot who appears first in Les Chouans and then, in terms of publication, fifteen years later in La Cousine Bette. In the former, we see him as a sort of incarnation of the Republic: 'Il gardait une attitude prophétique et apparaissait là comme le génie même de la Bretagne [he maintained a prophetic attitude and appeared as if he were the very genius of Britainy]' (viii, 916), allegiance firmly with France irrespective of the leader, and who despises those whose allegiance appears somewhat suspect. He calls Corentin, 'Le diable [qui] s'est fait homme [the devil who has made himself human]' (viii, 1185) and despises those of a similar ilk. In La Cousine Bette, however, we see him in a different light: now renowned as a war hero ('les sympathies populaires dans tout le quartier [the popular support of the whole neighbourhood]' (CB, 338)) and having accumulated a good fortune, he is his brother's saviour, wanting to protect the family name from disgrace: 'je ne veux pas qu'il y ait dans la fortune de la famille Hulot un liard de volé dans les deniers de l'État [I don't want the Hulot family's fortune to include a penny stolen from the public purse] ' (CB, 353). He pays off the debt incurred by his brother, covering it up in a surreptitious, not wholly legitimate way. We therefore see both his consistent and changing characteristics in different situations: first fighting for France and then for his family name. By recognising that a character's 'histoire' is in fact a cycle of 'histoires', Balzac questions history's objectivity and thereby mimics the anachronistic experiences of real life.

Moreover, in La Cousine Bette, Hulot's brother, Baron Hulot, represents the decreasing fortune of the Hulot family as they fail to adapt to the new regime and this is juxtaposed with Célestin Crevel, the rising bourgeois, the parvenu who adapts to changing history. Lukacs notes: 'Balzac utilise le personnage tout aussi magistral de Crevel comme contraste pour souligner l'opposition entre l'érotisme napoléonien et l'érotisme louis- philippard [Balzac uses the equally masterful character of Crevel as a contrast to underline the opposition between Napoleonic and Louis-Philippe eroticism]'. Indeed, Crevel says: 'Depuis que je n'ai mis les pieds chez vous [Adeline], vous n'avez pas pu renouveler le meuble de votre salon [Since I've been in your [Adeline's], house you haven't been able to renew the furniture in your living room]' (CB, 43) and later, Adeline notes the contrast of her former life with the luxury that Josepha, and other courtesans, now enjoy: '[Adeline] vivait au milieu des froides reliques du luxe impérial [...] entrevit la puissance des seductions du Vice en en voyant les résultats [Adeline] lived amidst the cold relics of imperial luxury [...] glimpsed the power of seductions of Vice by seeing the results]' (CB, 380). It is, however, Crevel who ultimately 'wins' Mme Marneffe, the prize over which the two men fight, and Hulot, 'Cet homme de l'Empire, habitué au genre Empire, devait ignorer absolument les façons de l'amour modern [This man of the Empire, accustomed to the Empire genre, must have been completely ignorant of the ways of modern love]'(CB, 121), is left in the past. Thus, by tracing the history of a family from one of Balzac's first novels to one of his last, we see the importance of historical change and how its effects on characters over time becomes the key to the 'Histoire secrète', enabling the author to express judgement on men, events and the process of history itself in his fictional vérité.

This interest in subjective history becomes pivotal to Balzac's creation. His so called 'historical novel' (Les Chouans) becomes more complicated when the author writes in the Avertissement du Gars that it is not a historical novel according to the 'règles de ce genre de composition [rules of this type of composition]' (viii, 1676). What Balzac means by this is that whilst his novel may be set in a historical period, it is not reliable in terms of historical truth. Andréoli argues that this does not question the mimetic reading of the work, but rather makes the limits of mimesis clear. For example, whilst geographically Fougère exists and 'son château domine, en haut du rocher où il est bâti, trois ou quatre routes importantes, position qui la rendait jadis une des clés de la Bretagne [This man of the Empire, accustomed to the Empire style, must have been completely unaware of the ways of love his castle dominates, at the top of the rock where it is built, three or four important roads, a position which once made it one of the keys to modern Britain]' (viii, 912) is very much vrai, when combined with fictional characters and plot, the Bretagne of Balzac's novel becomes an 'espace imaginaire [imaginary space]'. The work raises the surroundings to the aesthetic and literary level giving chouannerie and Bretagne a status beyond historic and geographic.

Balzac also does this by removing one specific historical figure, the 'grand homme [great man]', and instead focusing on groups of historically insignificant people. In Les Chouans, for example, rather than the main, real political leaders of the post-revolution, we are presented with small groups of Republicans and guerrilla fighters in a seemingly insignificant battle: 'des gens qui pillent un coin de la France au lieu d'assaillir toute la République [people who plunder one corner of France instead of assaulting the whole Republic]' (viii, 1038). Whilst Napoleon is mentioned ('le bruit du magique retour du general Bonaparte et des événements du Dix-huit Brumaire ne tarda pas à se répandre [the rumour of the magical return of general Bonaparte and the events of the Eighteenth of Brumaire did not take long to spread]' (my italics) (viii, 957)), his presence remains rather ghost-like and allows Balzac the freedom to play with the imaginary. Napoleon does, however, figure in Une ténébreuse affaire [A Murky Business]. Here, though, he destroys the 1804 conspiracy with the help of Fouché, the prime mover, and when Laurence comes face to face with him, he appears on the same plane as her: 'Vous êtes une femme, dit-il avec une teinte de raillerie. – Et vous un homme de fer! [You are a woman," he said with a tinge of mockery. - And you are an iron man!]' (viii, 681). She sees in Napoleon not a historical figure, but a human who has similarities with herself i.e. is a fictional character. It is, therefore, the idea of Napoleon that is important rather than his dramatic role. It is the human interest, 'cette histoire du cœur humain [this story of the human heart]' (i, 10), not history in its textbook form, that interests the visionary and, therefore, Balzac. Thus, whilst Scott has a greater propensity to use the 'grand homme', such as Richard the Lionheart or Bonnie Prince Charlie, to reveal the 'esprit d'une époque' (viii, 897) for Balzac what is important is the way the 'esprit' (viii, 897) is revealed in the entirety of the work, in the 'système' he creates. In short, the vrai is extrapolated into the fictional, revealing a fresco of society.

For Balzac, then, it is minor, fictional players facing random occurrences which take the limelight and through these that he focalises the history of the period, arguably the foundation of the Realist mode. For example, the Napoleonic myth is visible in the likes of Lucien and Rastignac, their sexual and social arrivisme and their turmoil as they strive for their own destiny e.g. Lucien's returning from Paris to Angoulême in Part III of Illusions perdues, or even in the description and the rising 'ruche [hive]' (PG, 313) full of the worker bees heading towards industrialisation that imply Rastignac's own advancement. What is created, then, instead of individual characters is the idea of the type, binding the general and the particular, and producing a portrayal of the complete human personality. The historical 'grand homme' is a bad novel character because, as an individual, 'il excède par trop la catégorie du typique [He too much exceeds the category of the typical]'. By dispensing of that individual, local dramas become generalised into an illustration of the interplay of broader social and historical forces. As Balzac writes: 'Il n'y a rien qui soit d'un seul bloc dans ce monde, tout y est mosaïque [There is nothing that is a single block in this world, everything is mosaic.]' (ii, 265): the individuals come together and the story of, say, Félix Grandet's avarice becomes typical of contemporary French society, whilst he is actually only a fictional character.

Balzac looks beyond historical accuracy to the philosophical and moral causes and consequences of events. In Les Chouans, a work known as 'historical' as it is framed by the royalist/republican feud, at its core is a love story between Montauran and Marie and how the couple is ruined and eventually destroyed by the vicissitudes of the revolt. It is this couple's adaptation to changing history rather than history itself that is the focus. For example, Marie is led throughout the novel by her emotions, at first the need to deceive Montauran, showing her true self in a dramatic, frantic revelation: 'Tout ce que vous avez soupçonné de moi est vrai! [Everything you have suspected about me is true]' (viii, 1143) and working for the reward of 'trois cent milles francs [three hundred thousand francs]' (viii, 1067). When dancing with Montauran, though, she feels 'tous les plaisirs qu'ils espéraient d'une plus intime union [all the pleasures they could hope for from such an intimate union]' (viii, 1142). It is her passion that leads her and as Balzac tells us: '[l]a passion est toute l'humanité. Sans elle, la religion, l'histoire, le roman, l'art seraient inutile [Passion is all humanity. Without it, religion, history, the novel, art would be useless'.]' (i, 14). Unfortunately, the other aristocratic leaders as well as Corentin, the shifty spy, are also led by their passions and desire for personal gain, and this conflict contributes to the death of the lovers. Corentin wants success and money 'il n'y a pas d'amour qui vaille trois cent mille francs [no love is worth three thousand francs]' (viii, 1067) and says that we will 'Employer habilement les passion des hommes ou des femmes comme des resorts que l'on fait mouvoir au profit de l'État [Skillfully use the passions of men or women as resources to be moved for the benefit of the state]' (viii, 1148) as justification for personal gain. His scheming, though, ends with the death of Marie as he lacks the selfless devotion to a general cause. Ultimately, Marie's rejection of Corentin ('la constante répugnance que vous m'inspirez [the constant repugnance that you have created in me]' (viii, 1155)) and acceptance of Montauran, despite being on the opposing side, suggests that love is more important than war. Montauran even revolts against his aristocratic background that would prevent his marriage to 'an illegitimate woman with a questionable history', as Pasco describes. In short, nothing can compete with human passion. Furthermore, in the mini-epilogue, Marche-àterre, whose violence made him almost bestial (so much so that 'on pouvait facilement [...] confondre [...] ces malheureux avec les animaux [one could easily [...] confuse [...] these unfortunate people with animals]' (viii, 906)), has apparently become human: 'Voilà un bien brave homme! [There is a heck of a brave man!]' (viii, 1211). It is implied that he is changed by the love of Francine and has removed himself from society into a more noble state, no longer spending his energy on vengeful, power-hungry battle, suggesting that, whilst clichéd, human nature can win, as long as it is tempered.

It is human nature, placed on an historical backdrop, and the way the former reacts to situations that is put on trial in Balzac's novel. Rather than depicting the 'Histoire officielle', which renders history something abstract, beyond human responsibility, the 'Histoire secrète' reminds us of the causes behind it: human passion and both its danger and potential for greatness.

Just as the word vraisemblable stems from the word vrai, so too does Balzac's fictional universe 'stem from' the real. Instead of simply recounting history, the job of the historian, Balzac acts as translator, as 'visionnaire' as Baudelaire argues, extrapolating from the 'histoire officielle', that of abstract history told in textbooks, to the 'histoire secrète' that includes the real motivations of human life. Indeed, if Balzac is to be considered a visionary it is in this sense: a seer of human nature.

### Primary Sources

Balzac, Honoré de, La Comédie humaine, ed. Pierre-Georges Castex et al, Nouvelle edition, 12 vols. (Paris: Gallimard, 1976-1981).

PG: Balzac, Honoré de, Le Père Goriot, ed. Philippe Berthier and Nadine Satiat (Paris: Flammarion, 1995, updated 2006).

CB: Balzac, Honoré de, La Cousine Bette, ed. Pierre Barbéris IParis: Gallimard, 1972).

# PLEASURABLE READING

*BY STEPHANIE MARRIE*

When one opens a book about pleasure, they are being invited to bed. Unless the book lets reader inside, they cannot make love. To accomplish this, three significant books manipulate the reader's love of watching, or scopophilia in Freud's terms. The effect of the book's characters' actions and settings on the reader is perfectly encapsulated in this quote from Times square red, times square blue by Delaney, wherein the narrator masturbates to a gorgeous young man masturbating to a woman in a porn film: "I'm getting' off on her up there-" he pointed at the screen-"and you guys are all getting' off on me...?" (22). "Rape of the Lock" gives the reader a peek into a woman's private space and then her headspace. "The Picture of Dorian Gray" gives reader a peek into a man's room and his headspace. Only "Vox" balances its gaze by giving reader a peek into both a male and female headspace. Male authors, however, have written all three books. As demonstrated by Nicholson Baker's "Vox," Oscar Wilde's "The Picture of Dorian Gray," and Alexander Pope's "The Rape of the Lock," albeit through different means, a book about pleasure has to bring the reader inside its body in order to be satisfying.

A book on pleasure is successful at seducing the reader via meticulous scene setting and vivid language. Pope's details take the reader back to the 18th century fashion world, where the social boundary between upper class men and women were becoming increasingly blurred (6). Since the historical background of his poetry is characterized by "boundary crossings" (10), it's even more fitting that the reader is allowed to cross the boundary of reality in order to ogle a fictional woman. The interplay of seduction and language within the narrative is characteristic of the post-Restoration, 17th century English social climate "charged with verbal wit and sexual energy," when the theatres reopened (7). As the actors charmed audiences with those two elements, so does Pope for the readers in order to absorb them into his fictional world.

What the reader delights in here is the rare chance to see "things not understood by the mob," as Mandeville would say, such as an upper class lady's "private diversions, the pomp and luxury of the dining room and the bed-chamber", and the "curiosities" of her closet (92). In the first canto of "The Rape of the Lock," the reader is given a peek into Belinda sleeping:

*"The Morning-Dream that hover'd o'er her Head. / A Youth more glitt'ring than a Birth-night Beau, / (That ev'n in Slumber caus'd her Cheek to glow) / Seem'd to her Ear his winning Lips to lay, / And thus in Whispers said, or seem'd to say." (pg 53-54, lines 22-26)*

She is in the process of waking from a sexy dream, and though she outwardly appears as a chaste woman, the reader is privy to her innermost sexual desires via titillating description. The reader does not see her dream man, but phrases like "winning Lips" and "Youth more glitt'ring than a birthnight Beau" make him appear seductive and almost makes the reader want to be caressed by him too. The rhyme reinforces his desirability, with "Beau" going with "glow" to the most satisfying effect. The effect may differ depending on the reader. If the reader is a straight woman, she'll wonder what the youth looks like. If the reader is a straight man, he'll delight in Belinda's resulting pleasure and imagine her cheek glowing if he were to hypothetically make love to her.

If her waking up is not titillating enough, the reader is then treated to a scene of Belinda making herself up:

*"First, rob'd in White, the Nymph intent adores / With Head uncover'd, the cosmetic Pow'rs. / A heav'nly Image in the Glass appears, / To that she bends, to that her Eyes she rears...Unnumber'd Treasures ope at once, and here/The various / Off'rings of the World appear; / From each she nicely culls with curious Toil, / And decks the Goddess with the glitt'ring Spoil. / This Casket India's glowing Gems unlocks, / And all Arabia breathes from yonder Box...Here Files of Pins extend their shining Rows, / Puffs, Powders, Patches, Bibles, Billet-doux. / Now awful Beauty puts on all its Arms; / The Fair each moment rises in her Charms, / Repairs her Smiles, awakens ev'ry Grace, / And calls forth all the Wonders of her Face; / Sees by Degrees a purer Blush arise, / And keener Lightnings quicken in her Eyes. (page 57, canto 1, lines 124-144)*

Belinda is made up as carefully as possible for the reader to catch every detail, to the point where they powder her face and fix up her eyelashes along with the maid and the author. The reader does her up vicariously through the writing because the details are so vivid the world and its circumstances feel authentic. The reader is not allowed to make up Dorian Gray in the same way, nor either of the main characters in Vox. This scene is as intimate and sensual as one can get without necessarily being directly sexual.

Yet the focus isn't Belinda herself, but the beautiful objects used to make her up. Thus, Belinda is objectified in a sense, but not in the usual way that the narrative pans over her body. Rather, she is objectified in the sense that she is a blank slate made the sum of outside parts, since a lot of the items are foreign goods like "India's glowing gems" and "all Arabia" from "yonder Box." Belinda herself has no agency, she does not make herself up, and it's not about her pleasure at being pretty but at the reader's pleasure from dolling her up. There is not much of a reaction detailed in the passage other than the maid intently adoring Belinda's face before she begins the routine. Belinda's not metaphorically masturbating to herself, but the reader masturbates to her. Imagine how the readers' pleasure will peak when they see the finished product!

The scene on page 106, chapter 11, however, is a metaphorical masturbation, but while Gray gets off on himself like Narcissus, the reader cannot get off on him getting off:

*"he himself would creep upstairs to the locked room, open the door with the key that never left him now, and stand, with a mirror, in front of the portrait that Basil Hallward had painted of him, looking now at the evil and aging face on*

*the canvas, and now at the fair young face that laughed back at him from the polished glass. The very sharpness of the contrast used to quicken his sense of pleasure. He grew more and more enamoured of his own beauty, more and more interested in the corruption of his own soul. He would examine with minute care, and sometimes with a monstrous and terrible delight, the hideous lines that seared the wrinkling forehead or crawled around the heavy sensual mouth, wondering sometimes which were the more horrible, the signs of sin or the signs of age."*

Dorian Gray is alone, looking at himself. This is Gray's private moment but he has some agency, unlike Belinda, so reader feels slightly less of a subject or a voyeur. There are not really any details that make this scene sound particularly titillating to the reader, no in-depth descriptions of how happy Gray feels as he looks at himself. The passage is less about the portrait itself and more about Gray's reaction to image and what he does with it. We do not get many details as to what the portrait looks like, unlike the scene with Belinda being dolled up.

Without Pope's pretty and meticulous word choice, a similar scenario does not feel as titillating. In a document called "The social World: Their Pleasures: Joseph Addison, From The Spectator, No. 323 ["Clarinda's journal"]," page 340, "Addison's satire exposes, even more than does "Rape of the Lock," the pleasurable vacuity that is the life of a fashionable young lady" but the way it peeks into Clarinda's life fails to satisfy. The format of Addison's text is a regular short schedule, nothing particularly titillating or intimate at all. A typical passage goes like this: "From Eleven to One. At my Toilet, try'd a new Head. Gave Orders for Veny to be combed and washed. Mem. I look best in Blue" (pg 341). The language is so cut and dry, and there are no outstanding details or vivid descriptions or poetry. Addison's piece demonstrates that a text on pleasure cannot be effective by just detailing what someone does for pleasure.

Wilde has as much of an ability to bring a reader inside as Pope, since he writes with "a fascination for detail," but unlike Pope who warned against the excesses of luxurious life in his work, Wilde apparently openly advocates for "a lifestyle based solely upon gratification, the New Hedonism expounded by Lord Henry" (xi). Even studying, never mind merely looking at other people, is pleasurable.

The only merely pleasurable moment in the novel comes from the gaze of Lord Henry:

*"And yet the lad's mad adoration of some one else caused him not the slightest pang of annoyance or jealousy. He was pleased by it. It made him a more interesting study...And so he had begun by vivisecting himself, as he had ended by vivisecting others. Human life-that appeared to him the one thing worth investigating. Compared to it there was nothing else of any value. It was true that as one watched life in its curious crucible of pain and pleasure, one could not wear over one's face a mask of glass, nor keep the sulphurous fumes from troubling the brain and making the imagination turbid with monstrous fantasies and misshapen dreams...And, yet, what a great reward one received! How*

*wonderful the whole world became to one! To note the curious hard logic of passion, and the emotional coloured life of the intellect-to observe where they met, and where they separated, at what point they were in unison, and at what point they were at discord-there was a delight in that! What matter what the cost was? One could never pay too high a price for any sensation."* (51)

This passage demonstrates that Lord Henry is the reader surrogate. It may not have titillating details, but it does have a titillating function: self-insertion. Like him, the reader is allowed to study this man from afar and admire the way he acts. The fact that the reader, like Lord Henry, is in control of the gaze brings more pleasure to the reader because he or she feels more powerful. It is a particularly pleasing moment because they see someone else having the same effect on beautiful Dorian Gray as he does to the average person: struck by another's beauty and falling madly in love as a result. The pleasure of the illusion of being in control wears off quickly, however, as we are never really given a chance to get intimate with Dorian Gray since he is fundamentally cold inside and spends his time alone. The more intimate with a character the reader is allowed, the more pleasure the reader gets.

The nature of Vox's characters is encapsulated in this quote:

*"Some people like spontaneous sexual scenes, others like highly scripted ones, others like spontaneous-sounding ones that are nonetheless totally predictable...For some people, it is important that sex be embedded in contexts resonant with meaning, narrative, and connectedness with other aspects of their life;"*

*(Eve Kosofsky Sedgwick's "Axiomatic:" page 325).*

Though none of these texts are about the conventional two-person setting, Vox has the greatest intimacy and thus the greatest titillating effect on the reader. In Vox, there is one man and one woman together, but not physically. There are different kinds of voyeurism in this text, including those of the characters, their friends, and the reader getting off on one another. There is an imagine and contrived explanation as to how Jill got her package: a few hot guys do the same thing one by one, they is some context given as to who the men are like their sexual orientation and their names, which all happen to sound similar.

In "Vox," page 14-15, Baker describes the process leading up to the tights and the check mark on the packing slip inside delivered to Jill Smith's that Jim ordered for her from Deliques. It is all being told via a telephone conversation between a man and a woman who have only just met. In-story, the whole scenario is Smith's imagination, according to Jim: a group of male models on the line pack her stuff in place of the older Laotian women. The event, as told by Jim to Abby on the phone, begins like this:

*"Looks at her name, Jill Smith, and then takes the order slip and crumples it against the piece of horseradish in his foulard silk boxer shorts, and he hands it to the next male model, a gorgeous peasant with strange slitty nipples, who*

smooths it out, studies it, squeezes his asscheeks together, and passes it to the next guy...each one broader-shouldered and sinewier-stomached than the last," (14) and then last one pries open the highest pallet with "Probably his dick," Jim muses, but then Abby cuts in and says, "No, no, with his powerful refined hands...his cock is pressing against the cardboard, pressing, pressing, and it starts to fight against the tethers of that codpiece," and then Jim continues, "Well, while he was gone, Todd, Rod, and Sod, and Wadd, the other male models, all heterosexual, have been thinking about Jill Smith wearing those tights and by now their bobolinks have all gotten thoroughly hard," (15).

What we just had here was a mixture of the male and female gazes, or at least a female gaze dominating the scene despite being told by men. The input of women's thoughts complicates the traditional male gaze. Though we know what pleases this woman, we are taken into the scene and titillated by it as well. That way, it doesn't feel like we've invaded someone's private dirty thoughts, nor are we turned off by what we think is someone's creepy fetish, despite some of the dirty language like "asscheeks."

Jim then reminisces about a scene from Disney's Peter Pan with Tinker Bell:

"She's got quite small breasts but quite large little hips, and large little thighs, and she's wearing this tiny little outfit that's torn or jaggedly cut and barely covers her, and she looks down at herself, s lovely little pouty face, and she puts her hands on her hips as to measure them, and she shakes her head sadly-too wide, too wide. Oh that got me hot! And then a second later she gets caught in a dresser drawer among a lot of sewing things and she tries to fly out the keyhole but-nope, her hips are too wide, she gets stuck!" the woman, named Abby, replies to Jim's description, "Sounds sizzling hot." (Page 36)

It's strange that Jim likes to peep in on women doing sexual things in private, but he should also delight in their delight too. He likes to peek without being a peeping tom. He's even said that his presence would disrupt whatever feeling of pleasure there'd be from such a situation. Consider Page 66: about "hundreds of female orgasms could be inferred from the books themselves-you didn't need to harass any particular woman, you didn't need to invade anybody's privacy,"

Or the passage on Page 75: "stories represent women and are therefore sexually charged for me, and in fact that's what got me so hot at Bonnie's Books that time, the idea that I was peeing in on a woman's preserve. I think I am slowly starting to understand why in general people would prefer written porn. It gives your brain a vaginal orgasm rather than a clitoral orgasm, so to speak, whatever that means." The guy read a story from a men's magazine once that had "the pretense that a woman was telling the story," which may as well be a meta-commentary on how Baker tells a woman's story through Abby about her sexual fantasies that all somehow involve pleasuring a man, whether it'd be some doctor or men in the audience at a circus. Jim continues, "the fact that it was written in the voice of this girl, so I could peep in on her mixed feelings when her top came off, did give me a huge...an unexpectedly large return on my investment." This last statement encapsulates the purpose of this book to the reader: "I guess insofar as verbal pornography records thoughts rather than exclusively images, or at least surrounds all images with thoughts, or something, it can be the hottest medium of all. Telepathy on a budget." It truly is the hottest medium; all private thoughts are open to the reader without them having to feel like they were peeping into something not for them as they might feel in a film, perhaps.

Or this: "Any woman masturbates anywhere, I want to know about it. No woman is anything but beautiful when she is masturbating." (123) When Jim hears Abby masturbate at the very end of the novel, the reader is witness to it as well, and gets the pleasure that Jim gets from listening to it.

Abby also shares her fantasy. She once went to a smaller-scale South American circus with some guy, she says Venezuelan performer during two other men drumming was "a woman spun hard balls around very fast on long strings...and the balls smacked against the floorboards in interesting rhythms around her legs, and she was streaming with sweat, and quite beautiful," "I momentarily wanted to be her, and while they were taking their bows I adapted my striptease fantasy, and I thought I was this woman in the black spangles, and I was spinning these balls very fast, faster than she could, so they were a blur...pieces of clothing, fly outward, somehow my whole outfit was torn in pieces from my body, and flung out into the audience, so that when the drumming stopped and I froze suddenly and made my trilling scream, I was totally naked...each man who caught some damp shred of costume was overpowered and took his place in line to fuck me," (129). At a glance, this seems like her getting off of herself, a self-objectification. It's a male author writing a woman's fantasy about becoming the object of a male gaze, which undermines the sort of seeming gender balance of perspectives a bit. If the reader is male, he can fantasize about this woman stripping as well and want to be one of those men who wait in line to have sex with her.

Throughout pages 147 to 162, the structure goes like this: at first Jim gives long descriptions about how he seeks out and lusts after her and Abby makes some quick additions or responses, but then she's reduced to reacting to his very long, dominating sexual descriptions and she is being turned on while he tells her what he's doing to her at the end. After hearing about a sexual encounter that the woman had previously with a scientist, he begins to tell her about his own invention invented from her description, a sensing device, "What it does...it simply senses the presence nearby of any intelligent strumming woman. It looks like an antique pocket watch, it's gold, with a cover, but when you open it, instead of a dial, there is this mysterious fluid," (147) "It's called the Bionic Mmm-Detector," he says (148).

He describes an imaginary scenario where he's using his device, he suddenly picks up sensations from a woman in a nearby building from her lighted window, goes in to check out where it's coming from, finds her "on your bed, ...and you're reading about a job interview in which the woman interviewer is sucking the interviewee's cock, and you're right in the middle of things," (149) Even towards the end of the story, it's mostly a male fantasy with some input but mostly reaction from a woman. He does the act of sex to a woman, and she receives mostly. However, in a role reversal of sorts, she is getting off of his pleasure, rather than him getting off of female pleasure. This is like the relationship of the text to the reader, the text does and the reader receives and is pleasured as a result.

Secondly, a book on pleasures is successful sexually via fundamental distance. According to Edmund Burke, in his "SECT. XV. Of the effects of TRAGEDY.", his definition of the reader's relationship to the awful stuff that happens to characters in fiction is as follows: "we shall be much mistaken if we attribute any considerable part of our satisfaction in tragedy to a consideration that tragedy is a deceit, and its representations no realities. The nearer it approaches the reality, and the further it removes us from all idea of fiction, the more perfect its power." "We delight in seeing things, which so far from doing, our heartiest wishes would be to see redressed." (page 2)

The most important component of this phenomenon he speaks of is on page 3: "though he should be removed himself to the greatest distance from the danger." "What numbers from all parts would croud to behold the ruins," about if there was an earthquake in London or something, "our immunity from them which produces our delight" about fictitious distresses, "that it is absolutely necessary my life should be out of any imminent hazed before I can take a delight in the sufferings of others, real or imaginary, or indeed in any thing else from any cause whatsoever."

In ROTL, on page 73, canto iV, lines 4-24, the following passage details Belinda's mental trip into the Cave of Spleen:

"Not youthful Kings in Battel seiz'd alive...Not Cynthia when her Manteau's pinn'd awry, / E'er felt such Rage, Resentment and Despair, / As Thou, sad Virgin! for thy ravish'd Hair...Here, in a Grotto, sheltred close from Air, / And screen'd in Shades from Day's detested Glare, / She sighs for ever on her pensive Bed, / Pain at her side, and Megrim at her Head."

The part about Cynthia refers to any lady furious when her maid doesn't put on her loose upper garment correctly (page 73). Here, the reader delights at her overreaction to one of her would-be suitors cutting off a precious lock of her hair at a party. The elevated language, intentionally likening her despair to some epic war tragedy, makes her as a character seem pettier. The reader gets the pleasure to laugh at her as a result.

Wilde's text goes perfectly with the sentiments expressed by Burke, since his text explores the relation "of art to morality" (xi). As Dorian Gray is looking at his image on page 89: "he thought of praying that the horrible sympathy that existed between him and the picture might cease." He is pleased with the way it decays, and this going into his room secretly to watch the paining and delight in the fact that nobody else will see it makes it seem like a metaphor for masturbation, since it takes place behind closed doors and was said to cause aging back in his time, "For there would be a real pleasure in watching it. He would be able to follow his mind into its secret places. This portrait would be to him the most magical of mirrors. As it had been revealed to him his own body, so it would reveal to him his own soul. And when winter came upon it, he would still be standing where spring trembles on the verge of summer. When the blood crept from its face, and left behind a pallid mask of chalk with leaden eyes, he would keep the glamour of boyhood. Not one blossom of his loveliness would ever fade...He would be safe. That was everything." This is a sort of meta-commentary on how the real-life reader feels for any character suffering in any medium.

On page 105, "In one point, he was more fortunate than the novel's fantastic hero." About an unnamed book that he reads, he feels the following: "It was with an almost cruel joy-and perhaps in nearly every joy, as certainly in every pleasure, cruelty has its place-that he used to read the latter part of the book, with its really tragic, if somewhat overemphasized, account of the sorrow and despair of one who had himself lost what in others, and the world, he most dearly valued."

Keep in mind the story "seemed to contain the story of his own life" inside.

Dorian inadvertently provides why a reader likes to read about bad things happening to others, on page 126: "I love scandals about other people, but scandals about myself don't interest me. They have not got the charm of novelty." This is why a reader picks up a scandalous book, their own lives are so pure and dull that they can act naughty by living vicariously through a sinner. As long as it's not happening to them, the story remains comfortably in the realm of mere entertainment and does not hold any strong ramifications for the reader's mind. On page 125, Dorian says, "I should like to be somebody else," and whenever a reader picks up a book, so do they.

Page 106, chapter 11, Dorian revels in his false sense of escapism:

*"He would place his white hands beside the coarse bloated hands of the picture, and smile. He mocked the misshapen body and the failing limbs." "He would think of the ruin he had brought upon his soul with a pity that was all the more poignant because it was purely selfish. But moments such as these were rare."*

Later, when he reads about the history of tyrants and the like, neither his own awful actions nor those committed by others bother Mr. Gray, but he gets off more on others who get punished for them. "There was a horrible fascination in them all. He saw them at night, and they troubled his imagination in the day." "Dorian Gray had been poisoned by a book. There were moments when he looked on evil simply as a mode through which he could realize his conception of the beautiful." (Chapter 11, 123) It's as if he can safely reprimand himself through other people, without actually subjecting himself to any karma. The reader is implicitly allowed to do the same.

"Vox" has no tragedy, but the distance between the reader and the characters enables the readers to perform the sexy stuff the characters do without doing it themselves or risk sexually transmitted diseases. The two characters never have real sex, only simulated phone sex, giving a double safety net for readers.

A truly pleasurable book will make love to its reader by letting the reader enter it via pretty-sounding details. It must be written porn essentially to make the audience come, and it must allow for a double-gaze as well for maximum satisfaction.

# OF FAIR MAIDS AND RICH MEN

## BY STEPHANIE MARRIE

The play The Fair Maid of the West by Thomas Heywood presents a skewed vision of darker men in the Renaissance era. The darker man is a womanish man, surrendering to base lust instead of manly resistance. The Englishman Spencer, Bess's husband-to-be, is away from her for most of the play. On her quest to find him, she meets a Moroccan king name Mullisheg (a bastardization of the name Mulai Shiek). Bess and Mullisheg, despite not marrying and coming from different countries, negotiate international relations via amorous love and flirtation. Mullisheg is Spencer's dark mirror image as evident through his interactions with Bess.

Mullisheg gets a kiss out of Bess the same way Spencer does. Though the kiss is technically chaste, it is the closest to thing a sexual favor that Bess will give the king, considering he is not her husband and is a non-white man. Admittedly, Bess gives out kisses regularly, according to Spencer. When Spencer is confronted with the barmaid's tawdry reputation, he defends her in a condescending manner:

> I have proved her
> Unto the utmost test, examined her
> Even to a modest force, but all in vain.
> She'll laugh, confer, keep company, discourse,
> And something more, kiss; but beyond that compass
> She no way can be drawn. (58-62, I.ii)

He has tested her chastity essentially by harassing her, even nearly forcing himself on her. She will not put out, so to speak, no matter how hard he tries to break her down. She just puts off his earlier advances with girlish modesty which is equated to the ideal woman. Evidently a kiss is not at all scandalous, even if it is the closest thing a man can get to having sex with her. By Spencer's standards, then, whatever Bess will do flirtatiously with the king is nonthreatening. Therefore, when the King tries to flirt with her, he is on the same level as Spencer before he successfully courted her. Bess, for the king's willingness to receive her, kisses him after he asks her for one, and he then says, "This kiss hath all my vitals ecstatic"(67, V.i). Later on, the King of Fez wants to kill a Christian preacher for trying to convert the Moors to his religion. Since Bess wants the king to spare him, Mullisheg says, "A kiss shall be his pardon."(78, V.ii). Then she replies, "Thus I pay't."(line 79, page 87, V.ii). This is non-sexual prostitution, though the man does not pay the woman. Instead, the woman buys another man's life with bodily contact.

Like Spencer, Mullisheg provides material possessions in order to claim Bess for his own. The king says to Bess, "Were't half my kingdom, / That, beauteous English virgin, thou shalt have."(lines 48-49, V.i) This means that if he can have her, she will essentially be queen of half of his kingdom. She could have half his estate, essentially becoming his wife. She can have this wealth because she is a beautiful virgin. Then later on, the king proclaims, "And ask of me, be't half this kingdom's treasure / And thou art lady on't."(83-84, V.i) In return for her granting him "full fruition of thy love," (31, V.ii), Mullisheg says to Bess, "Thy Negro shall be ballast home with gold." (37, V.ii). He phrased his intention to buy her with money in a way that seems as if he is granting her something, but he clearly wants something else in return for such a generous offer. Most likely, given his lustful nature, it would be unlimited access to her body. In this sense, he is no different from Spencer, who only really appears at the beginning of the play. Spencer gives a speech to Bess after first falling in love with her:

> Here be my keys; my trunks take to thy charge.
>
> Such gold fit for transportive as I have,
>
> I'll bear along; the rest are freely thine.
>
> Money, apparel, and what else thou find'st
>
> Perhaps worth my bequest and thy receiving,
>
> I make thee mistress of. (36-41, I.iii)

Bess is given access to Spencer's wealth and possessions before he leaves for the sea. He says this as if she were already his wife despite not marrying her until the end of the play. In this passage, it is all about him giving her things, not her giving him things. She is given permission to own his wealth and the means of unlocking his treasure. He leaves her behind and he leaves his money behind with her so that she is free to do as she pleases with it, but he has, in this context, allowed this arrangement as long as she is faithful to him. She only has to receive it from him, he is active in that he gives and she is passive in that she receives. He makes her mistress of property and gives her status. He turns her into something she was not when she was single - rich. She is here a girl worth gold, as the play's alternative title goes, but not the provider of gold. This speech is a kind and romantic way of Spencer telling Bess that he has essentially bought her body; he has exclusive access to her body and to her love. By giving her his gold, he confirms that he possesses her as a person and that she will only give her body to him and nobody else in his absence. He gives her clothes and money, making her the new owner of his property. In exchange, she vows to remain virginal for her white lover despite her occupation as a barmaid. For her black would-be lover, however, her gift is a mere breadcrumb of a sterile kiss.

This play provides the same relationship twice: a rich man bestows wealth and status upon a beautiful woman whose only worth is her chastity. Thus, according to this text, this is the Renaissance marriage market in a nutshell. Yet this relationship crosses cultural and geographical borders, suggesting that the rich man and beautiful woman bargain is universal.

# OTHER ARTICLES

# WHEN THE STATE LACKS, CRIME FLOURISHES: A PARALLELISM BETWEEN WARLORDISM AND MAFIA

## BY DIEGO LAUDATO

### Introduction

In the last decades the Nation State has increasingly lost its uniqueness as the utmost political institution in the world. In the current global governance scenario [1] state sovereignty results much weaker than before. Other actors emerged indeed with an effective role in the set of power relations which shapes the authority over a specific territory. This is much more evident in the African context. The process of state simplification in this continent coincided with the crisis of the post-colonial institutions. After years of dictatorship, wars, inner conflicts and social struggles, the general health condition of the African States has been in many cases almost devastated. There are plenty of instances in which social services and public infrastructures are basically absent in the daily life of population. From a theoretical point of view, the of lack of state services can be thought as a manifestation of the Hobbesian state of nature [2]. The failure of the State is indeed faced through the establishment of the so-called social contracts, which signed private and mutual agreements among people. Quite clearly, this kind of contracts is characterized by a high level of pragmatic individualism. Each individual is naturally interested in achieving its own private profit, even in this way it could harm the counterpart. In this way private interests become dominant over the collective ones. In such a scenario violent people and criminal acts find the suitable stage to flourish.

The criminal deviation of a society is a very common experience occurring when the state presence on the territory is manifestly weak. If this seems to be generally accepted in Africa and, more in general in the Global South, this paper actually aims to show that the Global North 3 is not devoid of this phenomenon. Alternative powers, emerged through violent and criminal ways, flourished in both the South and the North of the world. They actually achieve influential roles in the sovereign matters of the related states, becoming, even if in different degrees, proper actors of the global governance. Both Warlordism and Mafia organizations are suitable examples of this phenomenon worldwide. The comparisons between them is indeed the core of this article. Through it, we will show that the Staet's lack in providing basic commodities can lead societies all over the world to be subjected to the ascent of criminal powers. Notwithstanding, there are also differences in the development of these two phenomena, which will be part of the analysis as well.

## When the State lacks, crime flourishes: a parallelism between Warlordism and Mafia

Warlordism is a controversial concept. It has been defined in many different ways. Some analysts describe it as a sort of orientalization [4] of Western people, unable to define different political realities than the ones developed in the Western world. From another point of view, the historian David G. Herrmann affirmed that: Warlordism is the default condition of humanity. , marking the natural condition of violence that characterize the context of the state of nature which people experience when there is no State. In this perspective, Kimberly Marten's definition seems to be particularly suitable. She describes warlords as those individuals who control small pieces of territory using a combination of force and patronage [5]. Violence results to be the distinctive character of warlords. It is the their first and most important tool of power, marking the difference between them and other kinds of "local power brokers" [6]. Indeed every warlord could rely on its own private militias, through which that violence is expressed both concretely and as an ongoing threat against the opponents.

This definition though is not complete. In fact history is full of instances about individuals who have tried to achieve a sovereign role through the use of violence. In spite of this, just few of them can be classified as proper warlords. The discriminating factor here lies in the purposes of that authority. Warlords are indeed interested in accumulating private wealth and personal influence over the surrounding population. It is basically a private conception of power, in which the own benefit emerged as the only wished purpose.

William Reno, renowned scholar of this topic, underlines that warlords do not aim their political action in order to provide services and public goods to the population under their control [7]. There is no care for both people and the surrounding lands in the warlords' power action. In this sense, violence as means of legitimization par excellence is a telling evidence. Such indiscriminate use of violence actually suggests that Warlordism finds the proper conditions to develop just in those territory where the state presence is weak. Indeed according to the Weberian criteria of modern statehood [8], the use of violence is, with law, taxation and property rights, one of the monopolies that the State is supposed to hold within its boundaries. As it has been stated in the introduction, African States are particularly affected in their sovereign exclusiveness. Not by chances, this continent provides a particularly favorable context to warlords' development. During their violent rise, warlords establish an effective web of clienteles, which is at the very basis of their influence in loco. This kind of patronage is completely in- formed by personal relations. Warlords are used to continuously renegotiate their network, in order to increasingly empower their authority and in turn weakening the state influence over their clienteles. Because of this, governors are in many cases forced to bargain with the warlords the governance of that specific region. In this way they ought to avoid an inner warfare state, guaranteeing an implicit armistice in which warlords' authority is de facto recognized.

The last point actually highlights a significant contradiction. Because of their hostile nature, warlords represent a major threat to state autonomy. Nevertheless, rather than facing such a competitor, the State tends to accept the alternative power within its boundaries. In this sense, warlords are active inside the State and their influence is framed within the latter's apparatus. Establishing the negotiations in matter of sovereignty, the official governor basically accepts the very existence of the warlord and its authority among its clienteles. In this way, however, assuming its presence and allowing its criminal activity the State is in a sense complicit with the warlord itself. The latter develops indeed major political skills, focusing in particular on the manipulation and corruption of the state bureaucracy. Through it, it aims to exploit the local resources in order to increase its personal wealth. What emerges therefore is a two-sided relation in which the warlord is at the same time part of the state machine and its first threat. This is possible because of the different purposes of the two powers active in the same territory. Essentially, the very goal of the warlord is to feed its patronage network, achieving through it new personal profit. It has not at all state-building aims and therefore it is not interested in challenging the state's duties. There is no proper competition between the scopes of the two. However, there is instead competition in their influence over population. The warlord eventually coexists with the State as a parasite rather than an associate, acting in the same geographical space and dealing with the same population.

There is however a different scenario that sometimes could alter the relation between the warlord and the State. There are indeed many references about warlords active in Africa and other regions of the Global South supported by external powers, such as multinational corporations or even different countries. Among the others, United States seem to be particularly willing to pursue this kind of foreign policy. In the context of global governance such external patronage is part of the wider process of outsourcing sovereignty. Here the warlord becomes a tool through which a foreign power economically interested in that specific area exercises its own influence over the local resources. Avoiding the presence of the territory, at the same time the patron avoids major costs concerning military actions and the direct govern of the territory. The warlord itself, of course, is not a bare, manipulable puppet in others' hands. It does have its own agency in the power relations of the region. Through its private militias and the local network of clienteles it has its own influence on the population. However, it results to be not self- sufficient in the global governance scenario. In order to preserve its existence, the warlord needs to be supported by a patron, whether the State in which it develop or a foreign power interested in the area. Because of the private nature of the network established by the warlord, the alliances can suddenly change, altering the power relations of the area. Eventual outcome, then, is an ongoing instability, which challenge the very chance to start a secure process of development for the local population [9].

On the other hand, as this paper would show, the Global North has experienced a comparable phenomenon, i.e. the rise of Mafia-type organizations. Generally speaking, Mafia is a common label used to assign to every criminal organization, especially, but not exclusively, those that are set in Italy. Umberto Santino [10] specifies the definition. According to him Mafia can be rather considered as the winning model of the criminal organizations in the nowadays system of power relation, able to be simultaneously active at the local, national and international level. He argued indeed that since the Seventies the Sicilian Mafia, perhaps the first to achieve a step forward in the worldwide criminal business, started to evolve its economical activities. In particular, drug-trades became the most successful field in which it operated. The relative wealth collected through this deal was then reinvested in different enterprises, both illegal and legal. Because of this spread Mafia obtained major profits, resulted in major influence on the territory in which it developed. Quite soon the evolution from a pure agrarian connotation to a more structured businesslike organization led Mafia to run into the State sphere of action. As in the warlords' case, the Italian political class as well started to bargain with the mafia dons, establishing mutual relations between the two parts. The 1992-1993's "bombs phase" testified that the rapport has not been always pacific. Unfortunately, this paper cannot be the proper place to analyze in a deeper way this bond. However, it is part of our focus, which investigates the parallelism between Mafia-type organizations and Warlordism.

In order to develop this comparison, the analysis of the starting conditions is a working inception. Santino stresses the context of the 19th century's Sicily, looking in particular at the power of the Italian State in loco. As in the African context analyzed earlier, the state apparatus resulted to be particularly weak. Sicilians clearly felt the absence of the institutions, experiencing a general condition of poverty and scarce chances to improve their social status. In this shared feeling, local inhabitants found in what would became mafia dons alternative points of reference able to provide the needing facilities for their own survival 11. Diego Gambetta, major mafia scholar, actually echoes Santino's point. In particular, he refers to a specific commodity that the State, among the others, was unable to provide to Sicilians: protection. This is particularly fitting for this paper's purposes, since protection properly recalls the monopoly of violence. As stated before, it is one of those monopoly which the State should hold within its boundaries. In fact it is one of the lacks which defines its weakness. The emergence of both warlords and mafia dons indeed is a clear evidence of this. In particular, mafia dons were able to respond Sicilians' need of security for their person and their private property. Thus they acted as sort of guarantor, overseeing the commercial transactions among citizens in exchange of proper bribes. All of this actually set the best starting conditions for the rise of the Sicilian Mafia [12].

The are more similarities between Warlordism and Mafias. One of them is the organizational structure of the two phenomena. Both the two criminal powers indeed relies on patronage networks based on violence. As in the case of warlords, mafia dons as well employ violence as first tool to exercise their influence over population. The widespread presence they achieve in their territory challenges the state authority. Hence the respective State is unavoidably led to negotiate the local power with both, establishing in this way a proper relation. According to Felia Allum and Renate Siebert, who deeply analyzed this topic, this is a shared feature of the two phenomena, thus a peculiarity of Mafia-type organizations in relation with other non-specific criminal entities. Specifying previous Santino's point, the two scholars maintain that general criminal gangs basically deal with the same business hold by Mafias, like drug-trades, extortion and bribes. The very difference lies exactly in the mafia dons' capability to establish a mutual negotiation with the political class of their territory. As well as for war- lords, the bargain's final aim is to protect and improve their influence and economic profit [13]. Sicilian Mafia has provided a very suitable instance of this collusion, as the verified relation established with the Italian Christian Democratic party (DC) witnesses.

In 1963 Italian government established the first "Anti mafia Parliamentary Commission", publishing its final report just in 1976. The latter showed the whole of the contradictions about the work of the Commission, which alternated both explicit denunciations of the collusion between Mafia and DC's members and the attempts to minimize that bond. In the following years, the Commissions proceeded its job, more and more highlighting the evolution of the Mafia's role in the bargain. Indeed the more it acquired legitimacy in the relation, the more Mafia required direct agency in Italian politics. The result was the development of a criminal influence in the political sphere of the country, through which Mafia interests were protected and even sponsored by the government [14]. The "Andreotti's trial", whose name refers to the former Italian premier Giulio Andreotti, held between 1996 and 1999, is the clearest evidence of the State-Mafia bond. The result- ing data highlights, as in the warlords' case, the development of a two-sided relation between the two elements at stake. Mafia dons emerge as proper parasites, indeed exploiting the democratic apparatus of the same State of which they represent the first challenge. They need to act within the institution, corrupting the state apparatus to protect their business. In this way, the increase their authority, achieving more influence and therefore decreasing the state legitimacy in the power negotiations.

However at this point the two phenomena do not follow exactly the same path. In the switch from the original agrarian attitude to a businesslike organization involved in the global market of criminal commodities, Mafias achieved a new status, which is still missing in the warlords' case. Ernesto Ugo Savona, former president of the European Society of Criminology, ex- plains this evolution, defining Mafias as "transnational criminal organizations", i.e. organized criminal groups based in one State but at the same time active also in host countries as actors of the global economy. Through the power they initially collected within their territory and the economic links they have been able to establish worldwide, Mafias have developed an own agency in the current system of global governance [15]. On the other hand, warlords, even if involved in the power negotiations about their territory, do not develop an international influence. Rather they still need to be sponsored by a patron, whether local or foreign, to affirm their authority in the face of the related State.

## Conclusions

This paper has highlighted the consequences of a society in which the state presence is perceived as weak. This happens generally when the State itself is unable to provide those commodities and services needed to the survival of its population. People are therefore forced to face the lack of public facilities, looking instead for private solutions. The result is the emergence of a sort of state of nature based on mutual relations among the inhabitants. However, such private agreements tend to be informed by a pragmatic individualism according to which each individual is interested in achieving an own profit even if the latter harms the counterpart. This instrumental rationalism naturally leads to a criminal deviation of the society. In other words, the more one employs violence, the more one is favorite to arise in the state of nature imposing its own criminal authority. The criminal deviation of society usually achieves an organized structure. This is true worldwide, as the instance of Warlordism and Mafia have tried to show.

In Africa, but more in general in the Global South's area, this phenomenon can acquire the form of Warlordism. It can be described as the power of an individual who controls a territory through the use of violence and of a personal patronage network. On the other hand, in the Global North Mafia- type organizations, developed initially in Southern Italy, and then in many other parts of the world, shape similar kind of criminal powers. As the warlords, indeed, mafia dons operate by means of the same tools: primarily violence and clienteles. The eventual goal is also the same: gaining the higher influence and the economical profit possible. In order to satisfy this will, they both are willing to establish bargains with the State in which they developed. This relation is two-sided: from one point of view, these two criminal powers are part of the State, manipulating its colluded apparatus to improve their status; at the same time, they represent the most dangerous threat to state sovereignty.

These two criminal manifestations are not completely identical though. If the starting conditions and the typical tools employed in order to affirm their authority are similar, the dimension they eventually achieve once they are fully developed is still different. Through the evolution toward a businesslike organization, Mafia-type organizations have actually shaped their peculiar role in the current context of global governance. In particular, developing their criminal trades worldwide, Mafias emerged as the most important dealers for any kind of illegal commodities, and in particular drugs, at the global level. In this way, they have achieved an own agency that has led them to interact in the global power dynamics as autonomous actors. Starting from a significant local and agrarian level, Mafias eventually enlarge their sphere of action, entering first a national and then an international dimension. The same did not occur yet for warlords. In fact they are still anchored to their territory, of which they represent though major actors in matter of governance.

Stretching the perspective worldwide, however, they are minor entities, mostly related to more powerful authority. Whether it is the State in which they developed or a foreign power economically interested in the area, warlords are indeed always sponsored by a superior patron who has its own agency in the global governance scenario.

Final aim of this paper has been to show that the criminal deviation of a society is a global phenomenon. It takes place when a State is so weak to lack in its public duties. Because of this, the geographic dimension of the work has been more indefinitely possible, ranging from the Global South to the Global North. Nonetheless, Africa and its peculiar case studies still has a central position within it. The analysis of Warlordism, indeed, still offers particularly fruitful lines of research. In the criminal organization's universe, warlords' role is still developing. Scholars, analysts and even politicians are more than interested in the understanding of their authoritative parabola. In this sense, African warlords' evolution can actually modifies the current balance in the global political arena, informing new nuances about the relations between the local and the global spheres in matter of power.

## Endnotes

[1] A working reference to the concept of global governance is: M. Duffield, Global Governance and the new wars. The merging of Development and Security, Zed Books, London, 2001.

[2] This political doctrine has been explained in: T. Hobbes, Leviathan or The Matter, Forme and Power of a Common-Wealth Ecclesiasticall and Civil, Andrew Crooke's editions, London, 1651.

[3] As explained by Mark Duffield, Global North and Global South are not just geographical terms, but they concern mainly the social sphere: M. Duffield, Global Governance and the new wars, op. cit., pp. 16-17.

[4] Orientalization is a term derived by E. Said, Orientalism, Vintage Books Edition, New York, 1979. Within this book, Said described his idea of Orientalism, which is the patronized representation of the East made by Western people.

[5] K. Marten, Warlords. Strong-arm brokers in weak States, Cornell University Press, New York, 2012, pp. 3-4.

[6] Other "local power brokers", for instance, are ethnic and religious leaders who achieved specific authority within a region.

[7] W. Reno, Warlord Politics and African States, Lynne Rienner Publisher, London, 1998.

[8] M. Weber, The professional and Vocation of Politics, in: P. Lassman and R. Speirs (ed.), Weber: Political Writings, Cambridge University Press, New York, 1994, pp. 310- 312.

[9] K. Marten, Warlords, op. cit., pp. 29-30.

[10] Umberto Santino is one of the most reliable authors about Mafia and Mafia-type organizations. He is the founder and director of the "Centro Siciliano di Documentazione

"Giuseppe Impastato" - Onlus", a pivotal cultural center aimed to educate about the mafia phenomenon, developing an aware kind of opposition to it.

[11] U. Santino, Mafia and Mafia-type organizations in Italy, in Centro Siciliano di Documentazione "Giuseppe Impastato" - Onlus, at: https://www.centroimpastato.com/mafia- and-mafia-type-organizations-in-italy/ , last view: 06/01/2022.

[12] D. Gambetta, The Sicilian Mafia. The business of Private Protection, Harvard University Press, Cambridge, 1993.

[13] F. Allum and R. Siebert (ed.), Organized Crime and Challenge to Democracy, Rout- ledge/ECPR, Abingdon, 2003, pp. 1-3.

[14] J.L. Briquet,  Organized Crime, politics and the judiciary in post-war Italy, in:  F. Allum and R. Siebert (ed.), Organized Crime and Challenge to Democracy, op. cit., p. 169.

[15] F. Allum and R. Siebert(ed.), Organized Crime and Challenge to Democracy, op. cit., p. 7.

## References

[1] F. Allum and R. Siebert (ed.), Organized Crime and Challenge to Democracy, Routledge/ECPR, Abingdon, 2003.

[2] J.L. Briquet, Organized Crime, politics and the judiciary in post-war Italy, in F. Allum and R. Siebert (ed.), Organized Crime and Challenge to Democracy, Routledge/ECPR, Abingdon, 2003.

[3] M. Duffield, Global Governance and the new wars. The merging of Development and Security, Zed Books, London,2001.

[4] D. Gambetta, The Sicilian Mafia. The business of Private Protection, Harvard University Press, Cambridge, 1993.

[5] T. Hobbes, Leviathan or The Matter, Forme and Power of a Common- Wealth Ecclesiasticall and Civil,, Andrew Crooke's editions, London,1651.

[6] K. Marten, Warlords. Strong-arm brokers in weak States, Cornell University Press, New York, 2012.

[7] W. Reno, Warlord Politics and African States, Lynne Rienner Publisher, London, 1998.

[8]  E. Said, Orientalism, Vintage Books Edition, New York, 1979.

[9]  M. Weber, The professional and Vocation of Politics in: P. Lassman and

R. Speirs (ed.), Weber: Political Writings, Cambridge University Press, New York, 1994.

## Webliography

[10] U. Santino, Mafia and Mafia-type organizations in Italy,  in Centro Siciliano di Documentazione "Giuseppe Impastato" - Onlus,  at: https://www.centroimpastato.com/mafia-and-mafia-type-organizations- in-italy/ , last view: 06/01/2022.

# RAMA COLLEGE COMPOSITION - A GENERATION BOOK

### BY JAYATI BHASIN

For a long time, my father always used to say, "If you want to improve your English and clear competitive exams, then read 'Rama College Composition'. That is the book your grandfather studied from and got placed in the Ministry of Law, and that is the book I studied from and got placed in the Ministry of External Affairs." And I always used to wonder, what was so special about the book, which being a book of English composition, has an Indian name, and is preferred more than the Oxford books. Well, it always used to amaze me.

So, one day I went to my father and told him to give me 'Rama College Composition'. To be honest here, I did not ask for the book because I wanted to read or study it. I asked for the book so that I could dig deeper into its mysterious nature.

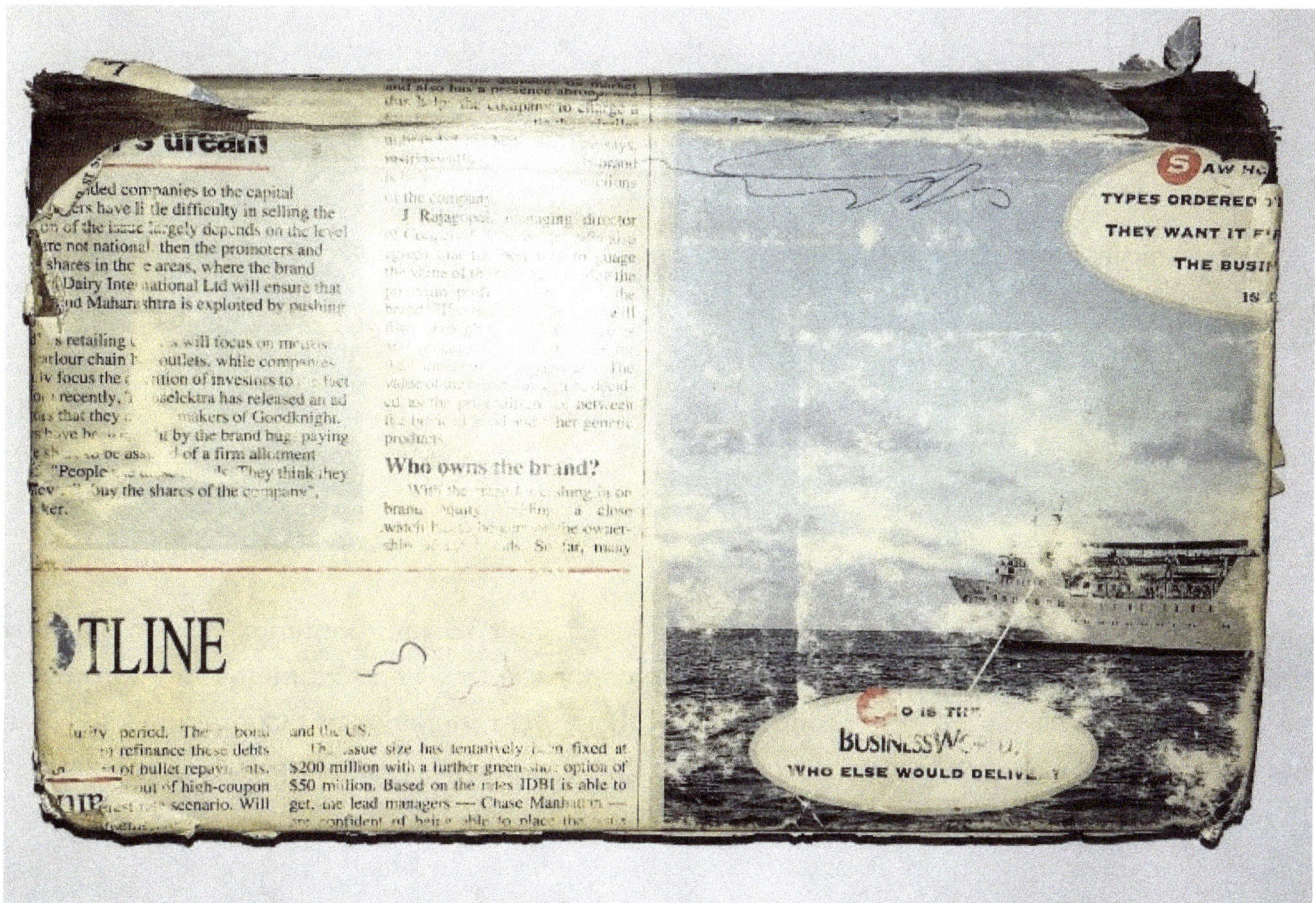

'Rama College Composition' book covered with the newspaper.

Once I received the book from my father, I was surprised by the condition it was preserved in. The book was covered in old, rusty newspaper, and at the same time, its pages were coming out because of the fragile binding. And as I was filled with curiosity, I opened the book and went to the very first page, where I saw my grandfather's signature along with the date. Speaking factually here, this is a common habit amongst readers; signing and writing the date of purchase on the very first page of the book.

Pages coming out of the book because of fragile binding.

My grandfather's signature along with date '23/02/60'.

Then, just when I skipped through three pages and went to the 'Contents' section, my jaw dropped. The whole content section had ticks, underlines, circles, and scribblings. Right from the very first chapter till the twenty-second chapter, there were markings of ticks, which I suppose meant that it was done; underlines, which meant that it was important; circles, which meant that they are yet to be studied; and scribblings, which served as short notes.

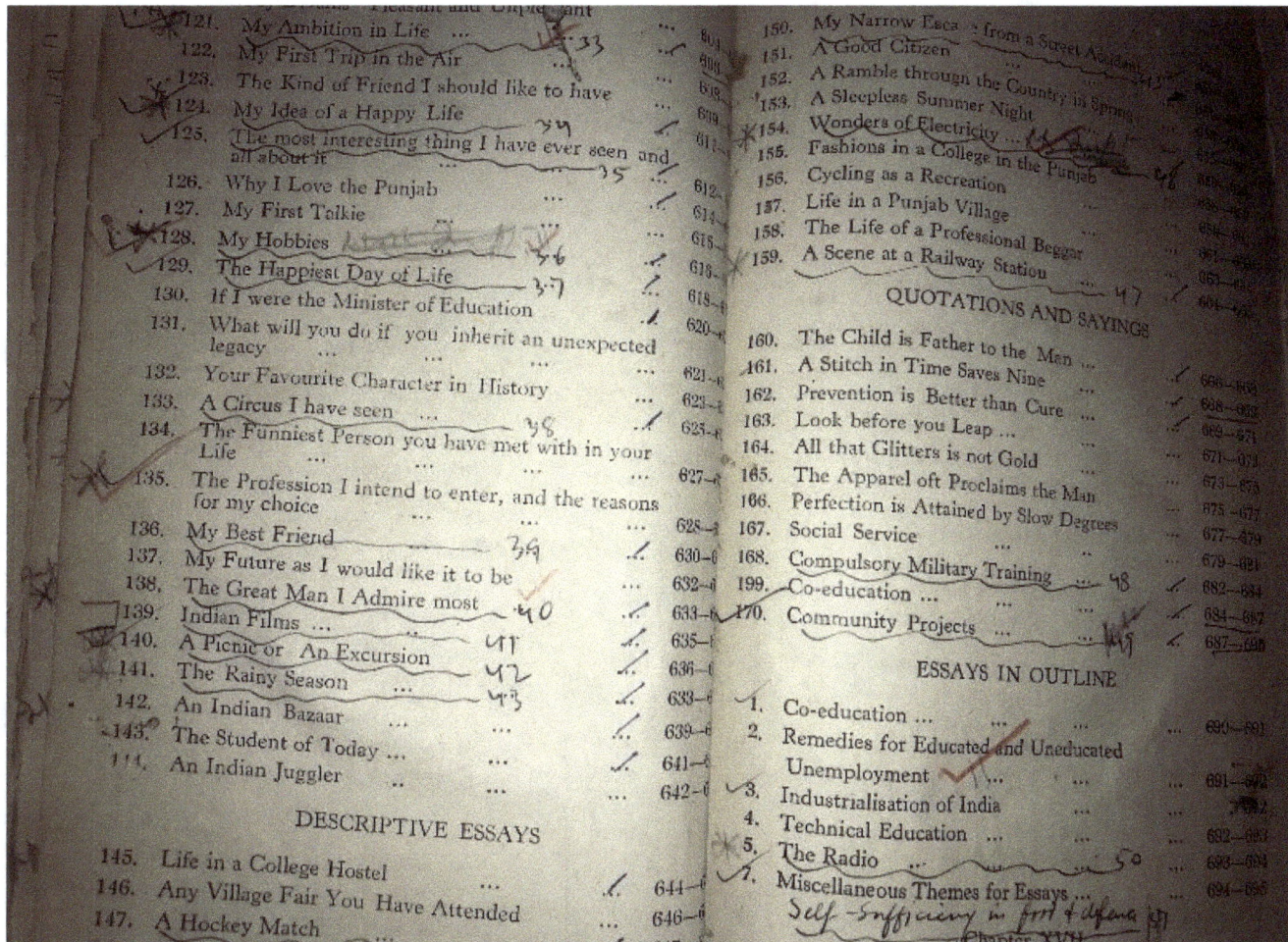

Ticks, underlines, circles, and scribblings by my grandfather and father.

Honestly speaking, by looking at the fox on every page of the book, I realised that this book is not just another book of English composition. This book, in our family, holds the same position which a bungalow holds on the document of testation.

Moving forward on the journey of unveiling this book, I started flipping through pages of different chapters. And while I was at it, I saw two different kinds of markings on the pages. One was of my grandfather, which was in the form of red and blue colour pencils and the other was of my father, which was in the form of lead pencil. Honestly, when I was finally convinced that 'Rama College Composition' is not a regular English composition book and cannot be compared with Oxford books ever, I saw something which made me realise that this is not the end.

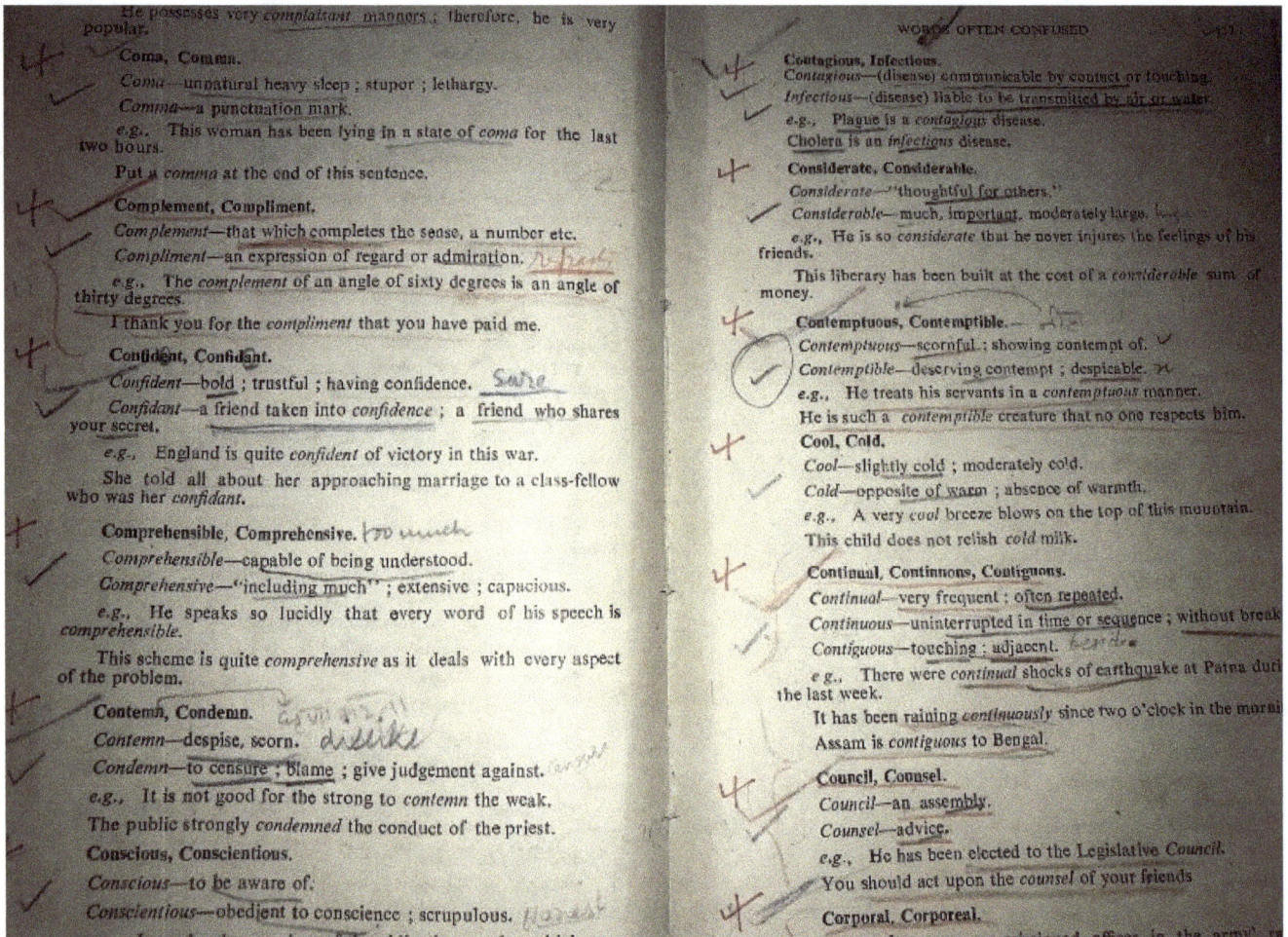

Two kinds of markings- markings in red and blue colour pencils are by my grandfather and markings with lead pencil are by my father.

While I was flipping through foxed pages, admiring different colours of underlines, and scribblings on top and bottom, I came across a few folded paper-notes which were written and kept between the book by my grandfather and father. One of them was a paper-note which was folded four times and my grandfather had written an essay on 'Students and Politics' on it. Another paper-note was by the name of my father and it was written with the help of a typewriter. In that paper-note, my father had written a letter to the Sports Authority of India while he was working in the Ministry of External Affairs, and showed interest in learning archery.

A folded paper-note on which my grandfather wrote an essay on 'Students and Politics'.

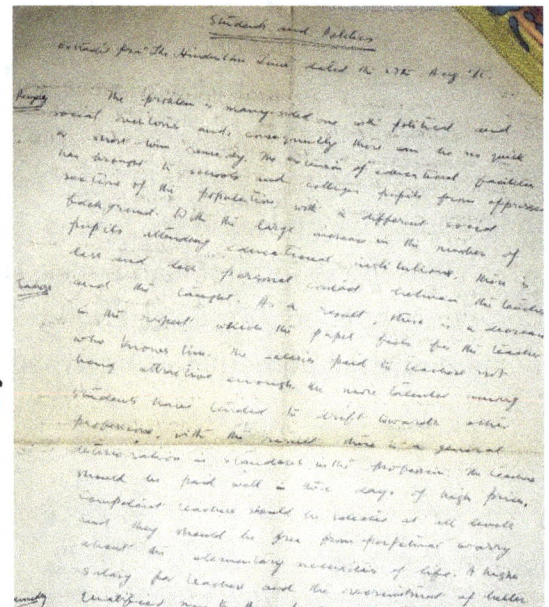

There were many such folded paper-notes in the book which made me discern as to how much of a student my grandfather was even after getting a job. And at the same time, how my father is no different than my grandfather and is still a student who studies till late at night.

Lastly, I think that the whole process of asking about this book from my father, seeing how it has been preserved till date like a gem, and going through all the pages and paper-notes, I've come to the conclusion that 'Rama College Composition' is no regular book in our family but is the 'Generation Book'. From being with my grandfather, to being with my father, and now being with myself; this book has undoubtedly served as a treasure which once belonged to the head of the family and is now with the current generation of the family.

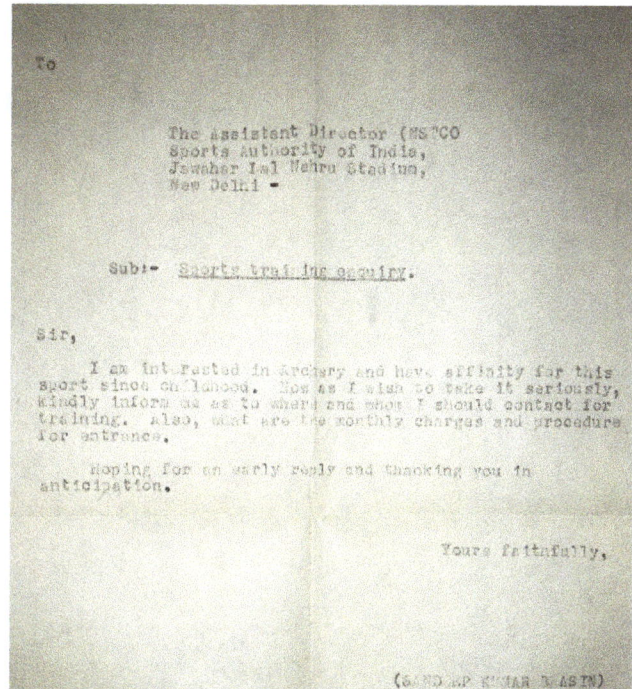

A folded paper-note on which my father, with the help of a typewriter, wrote a letter to the Sports Authority of India to enrol himself in archery classes.

# POETRY

# BUT AT LEAST WE HAVE MONEY

## BY MADISON LIPSKY

Trees of life will burn to ashes.
Flowing oceans of water will be poisoned.
Final breaths will be taken.
Precious life will be lost.
But at least we have money.

Beautiful animals will perish before us.
Our people will breathe fire in their chests.
The stars will disappear from the human eye.
Family trees will cease to grow.
But at least we have money.

The air will be contaminated.
The ruthless fog wont lift.
Icebergs will melt away.
Our children will suffer.
But at least we have money.

Cancer will multiply.
Hate will surpass love.
Intolerable pain will be inevitable.
Humanity will know no peace.
But at least we have money.

The Earth will expire.
Civilization will be lost.
An extinction of humanity.
The end of days.
But at least we have money.

# TWENTY TOO SLOW

## BY STEPHANIE MARRIE

Mountains of snow give way
to mountains of dead leaves
and freshly grown grass
through rain and shine

Up top, it's always winter
Down below, it's always summer
Snow and desert heat make me a trapped woman

It's a slow, boring game of Musical Chairs
Everyone dances the same way
to a robotic tune
until the coffee is ground to a halt
and we trample each other
until everyone sits on another's lap

My bagel is too soggy,
So my heart will wander
My fancy flies high above the stars
It is as powerful as my imagination
And much too free to be tied down
to the mediocrity of settling

# THREE THOUGHTFUL BEES

## BY BRONWEN EVANS

Berger, Baudrillard and Benjamin
all in their own way agreed
that reproduction mechanically,
mass production generically,
maps no longer exploratory,
our creation of pseudo reality
are a means to mere fantasy,
so nothing real again will ever be.
Based on symbols of what once was
a former time or style which came
not just from patterns but from the sub
cultures built from more than just their name,
streets based on streets from older days,
art robbed of its essence, how it was made.
When I see a photo, do I see a memory?
Or have I just made a new one
reminding me to remember the sea
that spurred the urge of photography.
And why is it that men decided
if we are to be ok with a woman's nudity
and in what situation.
It is ok to pose for a man for a painting
but hand me a mirror and it is vanity.
Fake morals
and fake towns,
a metaverse in earthy 3D
in what some would already agree
is a simulation, no will free.
Time and again I go back to these three
who join us in wondering
what our life would be
if progress wasn't agreed upon as technology.
Though with them I cannot always agree.

To take a photo and hang a print

may rid me of exact memory, the artist's authenticity

but without these things is it just kings

who would see art or earth in it's finery?

And without my map where would I be?

Lost on those newer older streets.

Though they foresaw what's happening now

the curse of great philosophy,

to see the great wave crashing down,

forced to live near the sea-soaked beach.

# ENTERTAINMENT

*BY NETA SHLAIN*

Stories told by
Smiles plastered
across faces,
Like rippling flags,
begging to see their eyes

There, plots vary
Oftentimes, from sad
To fearful, with the added lip bite,
A quick side glance
With a passing twitch

The personas altogether
Are relevant characters,
Plausible, palatable,
Relatable, likeable
For audiences sake

And viewers' delight
For the most part
Quite convincingly
On national television
and beyond

SHORT STORY

# THE CONSTRUCTION OF SPRING

*BY ZARA MENHENNET*

Beneath the morning's icy breath lies a glimmer of hope.Dawn's light has not yet escaped the sun to filter our sphere as the early twilight blankets cities, land and sea, but the morning star shines to let us know she is retiring from sight.

Out to the East, the Fire Temple of Baku dances a silhouette as the first rays of daybreak ripple across the Caspian Sea. Spreading outwards, it washes the Caucacus Mountains of Georgia to the north, while it wakes the silk merchants of Tabriz to the south. Rolling on, the pinks and reds now sprint the Black Sea, the violet sky overhead pale and cold as dawn wipes its sleepy eyes of blue. Temples in Istanbul glow bronze and the spires of Romanian chateaus gleam, the Pantheons of Greece defrost and the forests of Hungary shake off the heavy snow. Winter holds tight, despite the efforts of spring to break forth. The bears still sleep and mothers wait to bring young into the world. For you see, before cubs can run wild and the birds fly high, spring must be constructed, built piece by piece by those who we do not see...

Like every well-structured society, each individual has a role, a place to be and a task to perform. This too can be said for the Grasslings. Living deep in the earth, their labyrinth spreads far and wide beneath our world.The dark is their friend and the soil their lover, for no Grassling is truly at peace unless they are bettering the face of the earth. Worshippers of the sun, they prefer the cover of darkness, for the glowing orb is a powerful goddess, and too long in her presence burns their wings to a crisp.Their skin dark, they blend with the earth, hidden from our eyes that we may never find them, and working by night, they construct the glory and glamour of spring.

Orquidea, one of five daughters is one such Grassling.Born forth, it is her duty to cut free any buds or new leaves that are battling to shoot, otherwise known as a New Shoots Aid Worker. Her eldest sister, Violet, carries the charge of Emergency Plant Medic. Her primary job if to cover and heal any broken branches or off shoots that may have been broken by beings of the world above.Second and third born, Marigold and Hibiscus, joined the Plant Forces, protection of flowers against unwanted and deadly adversaries, while her youngest sister, Lilac, works in Plant Maintenance and Services. Each role is vital to the construction of spring, and even though at times it can be hard work, it is always rewarding.

Men and women are treated as equals in the Grassling society, neither seen as superior or earning more seeds of merit than the other.All positions of status are shared by both sexes while those of combat welcome all to their ranks. Bee Whisperers are generally women, simply as the hereditary gene required runs in the X chromosome, whereas Spider Gatherers and Worm Linguas run in the Y.That aside, Orquidea had always dreamed of being a Bee Whisperer, her grandmother having been one. The beauty of mounting such a beast in order to check the dew drops formed in the morning twilight, excited her imagination. To fly upon the back of a bumblebee to such heights, seeing the world at large, and the sun's rays before they hit the soil...

'Daydreaming, again?'

Orquidea flinched, her black eyes focusing on the dark, oval face before her. 'No.'

'Yes, you were,' poked her younger sister, Lilac. 'I bet is was about Cactai.'

Cactai was from another Grassling family. Built strong and tall, he overshadowed all others in the realm. His muscular body gleamed beneath the moonlight as he scaled ladders made of spider's silk, and swung his thorn sword with speed. First born, and having inherited the Y chromosome, he spent his nights with the other Spider Gatherers, a both violent and dangerous job.

'Actually, I was thinking of grandmama. And when she was a Bee Whisperer.'

'Not that, again! We've been through this; you didn't get the gene. None of us did.'

Scowling, Orquidea rested her chin on her knees, her wings fluttering slightly at her back. She hadn't slept a wink that day and reaching late-afternoon, was in for a rough night.

'Look!' exclaimed Lilac. 'There's Cactai, out with the others in broad daylight! You see, he can do it. Like grandmama he has the gene that allows him to face the Goddess's heat. You and I can't, we must accept that we are children of moonlight and shadow.'

Orquidea watched beside her sister as Cactai, with a small troop circled the stems, kicking off unwanted strays. Dusk was setting and winter's grip had not yet released, the sun watery and tepid. But she knew what Lilac meant, the sun was not her friend, like it was his.

'Come, we must get ready. We are on first rota tonight.' Called Lilac, walking off. Wiping her eyes, Orquidea followed, her sleek silhouette casting little shadow against the light that filtered in.

Now, Grasslings do not wear clothes, their smooth bodies being one with the earth, they sleep in discarded cocoons, and use preserved petals for wash basins. Fire flies and glow worms light their halls while tamed bumblebees shed hairs to fill their pillows.

Staring at her reflection in a dewdrop, Orquidea washed her face and slipped on her grass hoister, cutters hanging at her side. Pride swelled in her breast as she walked out into the evening, the sun completely set and a northerly breeze that promised a morning frost. There was work to be done.

Shouts could be heard of a young lieutenant who ran to the front – a frost was promised, a terrible frost! Word had reached the hub in the earth from a Grassling city up north, that temperatures had plummeted, killing many in their pursuit of a beautiful spring, frozen in time by the icy cold of early morning.

'I don't want to go,' cried Lilac, 'let's stay home and not go!'

'It is our duty to bring on spring,' she replied softly. 'Stay with mum, she needs you tonight. You are young, stay and be warm.'

Lilac's tears fell heavier than summer rain. Fear cursed her body as she hugged her sister who remained resolute in her desire to go. They parted, Lilac within, and Orquidea beyond the freshly sewn seeds to duty.

Painted in ink, the night sky sparkled with diamonds that reflected the pearly moon. So crisp, so clear, the icy shards penetrated Orquidea's lungs as she climbed the silk ladders. She sliced and cut against the growing cold, stems hardening as they froze. A cry was carried on the wind. Someone had fallen, their body freezing at the midnight hour.Hands clasping the silk thread, Orquidea inhaled the mournful cries that followed, howls of pain that crossed the sky like shooting stars. The wind now lifting, it engulfed her in fear, its artic soul grappling at hers.Her fingers felt stiff, she could climb no more. Did she shout? Did she call into the vacuum of the night? Tears froze on her cheeks before they fell, her body ached as she tried to move, her voice crystalising in her throat...Help...me...

It felt soft, the earth accepting her with open arms as her body lay strewn at the foot of the stem. She had cut, she had pushed against the winter forces to ensure another bud would grow. But now the stars grew hazy as the black night absorbed them, and the cries on the wind grew softer as she felt herself become one with the earth, no longer cold, numb without feeling. Her eyes eclipsed the moon and all was still.

Had she fallen? Did she now lie at the belly of the earth? She felt hollow, a shell abandoned for another. A voice rattled the empty halls of her mind, calling her name – Orquidea! Orquidea!It grew faint and then loud once more, a voice she did not know. She was weightless, held in the arms of some greater being as they carried her into the beyond. She felt safe, ready to go wherever they took her. A faint light hung above; an orb suspended. What was it? Was it the sun? Had spring broken winters grip and laid her bare before the heat that would devour her?

Her eyes snapped open. She was not dead, nor was she lying beneath the Goddess of the sky. It was a...a glow worm? A face loomed into view, a face she loved, Lilac's.

'We were so worried!' she cried. 'So many have not returned.' Orquidea's vision blurred. But how? Who? 'He heard you call,' continued Lilac, 'and carried you home.That's never happened before.'

All was a blur, a melange of sound and smells. She could see red, vivid in her mind's eye.

'Who brought me home?'

'Well,' Lilac stalled, 'a ladybird.' Orquidea's brain whirled in confusion. Grasslings did not converse with ladybirds, no one knew how to.'That's the thing... Cactai came across the ladybird as it was carrying you into one of the tunnels. He says you muttered something in their tongue that he didn't understand.'

'I spoke with a ladybird?'

'Yes.' Answered a masculine voice. Cactai had arrived to see her. 'I believe that's never been done before. You would be the first.' His oval eyes shone above his bevelled cheeks, a smile no one could read. He knelt beside her cocoon. 'When you are well, they want to see you in the centre hub.I believe great things lie before you.'Kissing her hand, he stood once more and left the room.

'Oh, my rosebuds!' cried Lilac. 'I don't know what is more exciting. That the centre hub wants to see you or that he kissed your hand!Cactai kissed your hand.'

Orquidea did not answer, but lay still, her mind fixed on red.Was she to be a pioneer in the construction of spring? Had she discovered a new gene that would allow them to advance the strokes of sunshine?

Outside, a new dawn was breaking, and the familiar shades of gold extended their fingers across the earth. Skimming oceans and scaling mountains, the morning rays pressed on.Reds and pinks once more painted the domes of Rome and the stone of Vienna glistened. Yet, the waves of yellow brought with it a new heat that poured through the Brandenburg Gate, and steamed the snow-capped peaks of the Alps.Dripping ice coursed through cracks of the Pyrenees, and the first flower slipped a tongue of colour to the sky.Spring had arrived.

# MARIGOLD

## BY RUBY EASTWOOD

The picture is probably all that survives of the place now, and it's a shame it's so grainy. Taken in the last of the light, the city skyline in the background is tinged with orange, but the block itself, with its unlit windows, is shaded by the more somber colours of twilight. The bell tower of a Romanesque church appears above the building, looking like a part of its design; whether intentionally or not, the angle at which the picture was taken has transformed the rooftop block into a strange, derelict castle, with monstrous black wires and TV antennae growing from its sides. In the eerie, crepuscular half-light of the photo, this illusion, which turns my father's crumbling attic into a fairytale palace, lingers somewhere between tragedy and comedy.

In Spanish, the name for the place where my father lived is palomar, an untranslatable word which literally means that it is fit for pigeons to live in. Through the long summer months, all the windows were left open, and I hung from the ceiling objects that would chime or rustle in the cross-breeze, thinking to make the place into a giant wind accordion. During the winter, the windows were shut but the wooden door would swell under the sea fog so it wouldn't shut, and the whole frame of the place seemed to expand and shrink like a breathing thing. To us it was not a place to live in but a place that lived with us, like the exoskeleton of an insect. I knew where the walls peeled, and the white cracked to show the layers of pastel pink and pea-green that through the years had been covered over with new paint. Hours of boredom had taught me to trace constellations across those walls; the cracks were rivers on an unsure map, and the stains like continents I couldn't name, or else faces speaking to each other across the room in a language I didn't understand. I knew which floorboards creaked, and which could keep a secret, and I think that if I shut my eyes, I might still remember the choreography that took me out onto the roof in silence.

Beneath the cramped garret was an even smaller system of tunnels and rooms, whose blueprint was unknowable and didn't accord with the confines of the rooms above. Only I understood the dreamlike logic of its interlocking chambers, and the low beams of the ceiling kept out adults.

This was the dark side of my father's minimalist life: dusty and dark, cluttered with bits of broken machines and curious relics from the streets, a labyrinth to hide the monster Chaos.

Sometimes bits of the mess would creep upstairs (they came in through the floorboards, or got out at night when nobody was watching) and over the years a circus of old toys had gathered in the house. There was a big blue eye, held by a curling wire to the top of a wine bottle, which watched over us, and a sad little Superman, whose once triumphant fist had broken off at the joint, and dangled limply. There were a few vinyls: Serge Gainsbourg, The Doors, Aretha Franklin and Leonard Cohen, but no record player. A desiccated lizard hung on the wall above the dinner table along with a dried up rose and a sepia photograph of the young Juan Carlos I (my father becameinexplicably dewy-eyed when he spoke of the King of Spain). By the bed, the wrinkled face of a marionette was stuffed into the body of an old piggy bank to horrific effect. My least favourite was the burlesque performer doll, with her freakishly thin waist, holding up her red dress to expose her fishnets and garters. The collection on the whole expressed a macabre sense of humour and a mind that delighted in whimsy but was helplessly drawn to darkness.

This disposition was the organising power behind the bookshelf (and certainly the only organising power in the place). He had Hemingway and Nabokov, Shakespeare and Cervantes, but the serious literature was stored in the less accessible corners, while the pride of place was taken up by Edward Lear's Limericks, Peter Pan, The Jungle Book, Ogden Nash, Alice in Wonderland, Le Petit Prince, Roald Dahl... My father used to quote to me from the children's books he loved; never, it seemed, for my enjoyment, but for his own. He wrote his own children's book called Gorble the Grook, complete with frightening illustrations, about a lonely man who lived in a high up tree house and drank too much beer (unsurprising that when scientists trained a monkey to draw, the first thing it drew were the bars of its own cage).

Perhaps it was the children's literature which had contaminated my father's mind with notions of heroism. His was a heroism of the wrong kind; a venomous mixture of the Spanish matador, the Renaissance explorer and the medieval knight. During the summers he would disappear to live out his Cavalier fantasies, and returned every time bent a little more out of shape, but with an unvanquished ego. Once he left to go sailing and wasn't heard of for many months until he showed up at my school gates in late autumn, with a big Russian coat, a gruff voice and three cracked ribs. I was pleased to see him, but my mother was furious, and his girlfriend, unwilling to assume the role of faithful Penelope, had found herself someone else. 'What sort of victory procession is this for a long lost hero?' wheezed my father.

He was a demi-god in his youth, he used to say (only half joking) and now, alone in his crumbling shepherd's hut on the mountain, drinking litres of red wine and looking up at the wind turbines, he fancies he is Don Quixote. He is Prometheus, too, though he doesn't know it; pecking away at his liver every day only for it to heal in his sleep. There is no water, or wine, on the hill, and when he goes down into the village and returns up the steep slope, buckling under the weight of bottles, he is also Sisyphus.

But it is absurd to compare my father to these tragic heroes; tragedy, as Aristotle conceives of it, is complete, brief, and grand. A spotlight on a dark stage, a milk-white mask contorted in a howl of pain, and a single action which turns a great king, in a blinding flash, into a beggar. Death is horrifying but clean, and is dealt with somewhere offstage. Next to the eloquence of this vision, my father's slow decay, the gradual glazing of his eyes and his ever more incoherent rantings, can only be described as a comedy.

When I think of the place on the rooftop, I return to the image of a diaphanous, white sheet hanging from the clothesline, and the memory of chasing its cooling shade as the sun drew its slow arc across the sky. Even now, barely four years away from the last of such idle summers, that way of life seems antiquated and fragile. I am almost surprised that the sound of drilling and destruction all over the city had never struck me then as a warning of the bulldozer which would eventually erase the place. I haven't been there since, but I'm told the building is now quite a nice hotel, with a swimming pool on the roof.

Throughout the months of legal struggle, my father's neighbours were displaced one by one, and the only light left on in the building was the little lighthouse of the palomar. Towards the end, when my father's grip on his home was slipping, and he would grope up the stairway in pitch blackness, past the bricked up doorways of his neighbours, the electricity and water shut off, it was unsure where he would go. More and more of his days would pass on park benches, and it seemed like a natural process of entropy would place him there permanently. My mother suggested the hut on the mountain, which though isolated and uninhabitable, was a more bearable prospect. When it was clear that the battle was over, she took him there on the train and left him on the mountain with a packed lunch. 'Even as a toddler you were never such hard work' she told me. He has written to me a few times and sometimes the skeleton of a leaf or a sprig of rosemary makes it in with the letter. Once, a golden marigold was folded between the pages of his spidery writing, perfectly flat, its colour intact. 'Up here there are two options' he wrote, 'to go insane or to at last become sane'. Though I don't think the latter is likely, it reassures me to think of him there, where time acts upon you in a different way, as if you are moving not through air but honey. I picture him sitting on my old swing, hearing the wind rush through the olive trees, or watching the eagle, with its majestic wingspan, glide across the sky over the craggy tops of mountains. In his letters, he meticulously documents the litres of rainwater that have gathered in the cistern, and I like to think of him in his solitude, counting each raindrop like a bead on a rosary. 'It is so peaceful' he writes, but really I know that it is a complaint; that he would give anything for the feel of concrete under his shoes, for the neon flash of bar-signs reflecting off windows, for the smell of sewage and cigarette smoke and the sound of laughter.

Until my mother dragged him by the hand and forced him up the mountain, he stubbornly refused to think of the future, as he had always done, surrendering himself to the clutch of luck. Instead of making plans, he accepted defeat, and drank himself into increasingly dire states. It was about this time that his obsession with the song Ziggy Stardust appeared. He would play it over and over on his old guitar, slurring the words and stripping them of all their rock n' roll. He took it all too far but boy could he play guitar… My mother's theory about why he would generally break down in tears just before that line was that he, like Ziggy, had taken it all too far, but unlike Ziggy, my father couldn't really play guitar.

What he felt was not sadness, he said, nor depression, but melancholia, a feeling infinitely more poetic. He said the feeling was black tar and treacle in his lungs and heart and soul, sickly bitter-sweet, sticky and dirty like guilt.

# ORANGES IN FEBRUARY

## BY ZARA MENHENNET

**Wednesday, 2 Days till Valentine's Day**

Ella sat staring at the orange half on her desk. Semi-dried out, she touched the red tissue paper it had been wrapped in, crinkling between her fingers.

'What on earth is that?' Chloe, who normally sat tucked in the next cubicle had stolen the first opportunity to see what the delivery had contained.

'I'm not quite sure,' replied Ella quietly. It came in the box.

'I take it, it's from Marcos?'

She simply nodded, still frowning slightly at the fruit.

'All that effort for half an orange?' chuckled Chloe. 'What did he think? You'd be hungry by eleven?'

Ella watched as Chloe walked off again, no doubt ready to sprinkle bits of orange grind gossip about the fourth floor.

Ella had been dating Marcos for just under two years, and things couldn't be better.He had not held back on meeting her friends, had jumped at the opportunity to meet her sister, and had even openly offered to meet her parents – something no other man in her dating history had dared do. Yet, here she sat, two days off Valentine's Day with half an orange on her desk.

Needing a coffee break, she stretched and made her way over to the Nespresso machine, and slipping in a capsule of extra smooth, rapped her red manicure against the counter.

'So,' sniggered a familiar voice, 'I hear you were sent a dried-up piece of fruit today.We are making leaps in the love department.'

Daphne, office co-ordinator and ex-girlfriend to Ella's ex. Ella rolled her eyes and forced a smile, clearly this was going to make it to the nineth floor before lunch. 'I did indeed.'

Daphne's eyes lit up. 'And it's true that it was specially delivery?'

'Chloe really needs more work to do, you know that?'

'Oh, come on!' she cried, clapping her hands together. 'You're the talk of the office! I've never seen anyone get an orange, sorry, half an orange as a gift before.Chloe couldn't help it, she just happened to be passing my door as I was leaving.'

Espresso ready, Ella raised an eye brow and moved off to the terrace, a small area where staff, normally, in summer months could take the air or have a quick fag.Right now, she'd face a blizzard if it meant putting distance between herself and Daphne.

Closing the door behind her, she cradled her coffee. Half an orange, she pondered. Marcos had always been a little special in her eyes. She'd met him in Madrid at a works conference during which time she was dating Ian – now also Daphne's ex. Marcos was Spanish, originally from a small city to the north of the capital, Teruel. Freezing in winter and baked in summer, Marcos had rattled on about this city that no one ever remembered except for the festivities in February – Los Amantes de Teruel. He had explained to her one day that they would go, as there was no festival more romantic anywhere. 'You see, Los Amantes de Teruel, or The Lovers of Teruel are a real-life version of Romeo and Juliet, and their tombs can even be visited in the local church' he would say, 'It's much better than Shakespeare!'.

Having been brought up in a modest middle-class family, Ella respected Shakespeare greatly, yet, had never had the desire to study him more than was required.Draining the last cold drops of coffee, she tossed away her cup and returned inside.

### Thursday, 1 Day to Valentine's Day

Climbing the Tube steps, Ella stepped into the bitter February air. Still dark, she crossed the street amongst the many commuters as they made their way to work. Lucky for her, the distance from her stop to the office was short with a Costa Coffee conveniently placed on the opposite corner.

Thank God for Apple Pay, she thought. No need to fumble with coins or cards – her fingers had stopped functioning when it had reached two degrees. Latte in hand she crossed back to the office and booting up her computer, was ready for another gruelling day of editing.

'How was the orange?' laughed Chloe, shaking off her navy coat.

'Ha, ha, ha,' smiled Ella. 'I have no idea what that was about.'

'You didn't ask?'

'He's at a work thing all week. No doubt there's some symbolic gesture behind it. I'm just unaware of what it is.'

'We're all unaware, dear.'

Disappearing from sight, Ella clipped open her compact. A set of blue-grey eyes stared back at her and her pale English complexion matched the office walls. Applying a little more blush and a spot of lip colour, she forged a smile at herself. The half orange had not gone far. It had merely travelled half a metre into her top draw out of sight. Clicking on the first email of the day, she pushed the fruit from her mind.

Time dragged when you weren't having fun, and to make it worse, the smell of orange had built up in the confined space. It was time to escape the desk, and pushing out her chair she decided to go for her morning ritual, an espresso.

'Special delivery,' called a voice. 'Letters and whatnot here in the collection point, and I need a Miss Stanley to sign for a parcel. A Miss E. Stanley.'

Oh God.What was it this time? Already standing, the last of the colour from her face reached her toes. Signing awkwardly, she pretended no-one was watching, and returning to her desk, found Chloe waiting for her.

'Is it Marcos? What did he send you? Come on, open it.'

Breathing shallow, Ella opened the box. Layers of pink and purple paper covered whatever lay beneath.

'I think I'll look later.'

'Oh no you don't,' snapped Chloe leaning in, 'let's see.'

Ella pulled away the paper to reveal a clean-cut half orange. What was this? Why couldn't it be a rose or chocolate? Not a bloody half piece of fruit!

'Another one!' cried Chloe, alerting all those within earshot and beyond. 'What on earth does it mean? I'm intrigued. I mean, the first one was simply odd, now its mysterious!'

Ella placed the paper back on top, closed the box best she could and slipped it into her second draw. She flushed red with embarrassment, not knowing what to say. Was he being romantic? Perhaps he didn't quite understand the concept of valentine's Day – after all, its not celebrated in Spain. Either way, her desk was filling with drying out fruit, her emails had accumulated and the entire office would now be informed of the second delivery today.Feeling a little down, she pulled out her phone.

-Hey, how's the trip going? I got your surprise box today...little confused...love you and travel safe tomorrow. Can't wait to see you. Besos. Xxx

Sent.She didn't want to seem ignorant, but couldn't ignore him either. Perhaps with this little push he might enlighten her to his unique way of expressing himself.

**Friday Morning – Valentine's Day**

Okay, so after all that, he still hadn't explained the two orange halves that sat in her desk. Multiple messages later, lots of kisses and "I love you's", but no insight. Today, was Valentine's Day and as the clock ticked closer to eleven, Ella felt herself entering the early stages of hot flushes.Ten years ahead of schedule, her body reminded her of the stressful event that would take place at approximately eleven o'clock each day...post. Perhaps it didn't help that she'd already downed three espressos and a latte before ten.

There he was, a box in hand. But before he could say anything she walked over to the collection point.

'Anything for me? Stanley?'

'Ah, why yes, this box. Need you to sign for it, please.' He pulled out a pen. 'Just there, in the square. That's perfect. Have a good day.'

He was gone and no one had looked round. Friday being their busiest day of the week meant all were occupied with deadlines and meetings. Slipping back to her desk, she looked to see if Chloe was about. Using her pen, she tore through the tape and opened the box.Once again, layers of coloured paper lay in the box. Closing her eyes, she breathed a sigh. Peeling away the papers, she found herself holding a whole orange – not cut in half – a full orange. Pressing it to her nose she took in its citric aroma, it smelt divine, the fruitiness reminded her of her trips to Spain, the blue skies and hillsides lines with orange trees.

This time, there was something more in the box. A business card – Con Estilo, Fusion Restaurant, Soho. On the back, 7:30pm, bring the orange.

### Friday Evening – Valentine's Day

They had agreed to meet there. For Ella, getting home, changed and out again meant 7:30pm was a squeeze. Marcos was already there, dressed in a smart black blazer, teamed with grey chinos and polished brown shoes. His skin sallow, the winter favoured him, and his jawline matched the strong wood cut of the bar where he sat sipping his drink.

'Sorry, I'm late,' she sighed, leaning in for a kiss. 'But really, 7:30 for me is impossible.'

'Cariño, don't worry about it,' his black eyes twinkled slightly. 'Our table is booked and I only just arrived myself. How was your day?'

She stared at him before answering. 'Not bad, I had another embarrassing box arrive today.'

'Embarrassing? But why?'

'You sent my two oranges halves and, thankfully, today a full one.' She turned to the barman, 'Dry white, please.'

'Do you have it with you?' asked Marcos. 'The orange?Can I have it?'

Pulling the orange out her bag, she held it out to Marcos.

'Dry white wine?' he asked.

She nodded, bewildered as he took the orange and passed it to the barman.

'Coming up.'

Ella watched the barman turn away to do her drink, there was something more at work here.

'I take it then you preferred the full orange,' said Marcos, bringing Ella back to look his way, 'so do I, we all do. Did you know, that in Spain, the orange is a really important fruit? I have told you before, Valentine's Day we don't celebrate, although commercialism is bringing it into the stores now. But the orange...now this is celebrated. We cultivate it and send it all over the world, even to your favourite, Marks & Spencer's. There is no escaping our beautiful oranges.'

Having returned, the barman placed the glass of dry white beside her, along with the orange that had been sliced. Taking no notice, Ella tilted her head to one side, unsure where this was going.

'There is an expression in Spanish, to be one's "media naranja" – half orange.When two halves come together, it makes the perfect whole. You are my media naranja, Ella.'

Ella laughed. She knew there had to be an explanation to all this! 'Ok, I get it now. But a little explanation before may have helped!I felt so awkward at work, and was made the gossip of the century.'

Marcos placed his hand on hers. 'Perhaps it was a little poetical, and one-sided. Here,' he gestured, 'have a piece.'

Turning to take a piece of orange, Ella stopped. There, nestled in the centre, sat a single diamond ring.

# Contact us

**This issue of Hermes Magazine is the final issue of this 9-part series. In 2021, with the cooperation of many writers, we were able to publish a thousand pages of articles, stories and poems. We are very happy and proud that you have read this magazine.**

You can contact Hermes Magazine in these ways.

Email:
Hermesmagazinelondon@yahoo.com

Website:
www.hermesmagazine.yolasite.com

LinkedIn:
www.linkedin.com/company/hermesmagazine

Instagram:
www.instagram.com/hermesmagazinelondon

www.ingramcontent.com/pod-product-compliance
Lightning Source LLC
Chambersburg PA
CBHW081539040426
42447CB00014B/3429